The Dance of Character and Plot

Author's Recent Books

The Survivor

The Chase

Under a Desert Sky

Pursuit of Justice

Sworn to Protect

Breach of Trust

The Dance of Character and Plot

DiAnn Mills

Bold Vision Books
P. O. Box 2011
Friendswood, Texas 77549

Dedication

Jerry B. Jenkins
and
The Craftsman Students of the Christian Writers Guild

Table of Contents

Chapter 1~The Beauty of Dance — 15

Chapter 2~First Steps — 20

Chapter 3~Breathing Life Into Your Story — 26

Chapter 4~Characters with Personality — 31

Chapter 5~ Deepening Characterization — 36

Chapter 6~The Dynamics of Setting — 42

Chapter 7~Plots That Dance, Part I — 49

Chapter 8~Plots That Dance, Part II — 56

Chapter 9~Point of View — 66

Chapter 10~The Dynamics of Emotion — 73

Chapter 11~Writing Dialogue that Sparkles, Part I — 84

Chapter 12~Writing Dialogue that Sparkles, Part II — 89

Chapter 13~Symbolism, Part I — 98

Chapter 14~Symbolism, Part II — 103

Chapter 15~Exposition, Narrative Summary,
      and Internal Dialogue — 109

Chapter 16~The Rhythm of Pacing — 115

Chapter 17~The Writer's Voice — 120

Chapter 18~Building Your Editing Muscles — 124

Chapter 19~The Tango of the Writing Life — 132

Resources — 139

Character Sketch — 139

Establishing Character Motivation — 141

12 Tips for Writing Strong Character-Driven Dialogue — 145

Four Essential Plot Questions — 147

Backstory — 148

Knowing Your Story — 149

Guidelines for Face to Face Critique Groups — 150

Guidelines for Online Critique Groups — 151

Suggested Readings — 152

Suggested Websites — 153

About the Author — 155

Acknowledgments

Lynette Eason

Julie Garmon

Dr. Dennis E. Hensley

Dean Mills

Andy Scheer

Introduction

I feel a thousand voices whispering to me—authors who touched me with their mastery of language and beauty; authors who taught me to imagine and dream; authors who taught me to create my own stories; and authors who inspired me to never settle for mediocrity. I've tried to pour their wisdom into these pages.

A voice in the back of my mind warns me about claiming any of their teachings as my own. I'm probably guilty. I've memorized so much from them, their gems have become a part of who I am. For their willingness to teach writers from the ground up, I am thankful.

Some teachers of fiction believe the novel is all about plot—that out of plot comes a character who has what it takes to reach a goal. Others, like me, have a passion for character. We believe that plot emerges from a character with certain wants, needs, strengths, weaknesses, and flaws.

For me, writing is an adventure, an exploration of what my character will do to accomplish a goal. I want to know these characters as close friends, to laugh, cry, and share the events of their lives.

From this philosophy blossoms *The Dance of Character and Plot*.

Let the dance begin.

Definitions

Antagonist - The character in story who opposes the protagonist's goals and viewpoint.

Backstory - The POV character's experiences that happened before chapter one, line one, that formed the character's personality and motivation in the story.

Character - A fictional person in story who is unique, compelling, and has physical and moral obstacles to overcome.

Character Arc - How a character changes and grows in the process of achieving a goal or solving a problem.

Dance - In the context of fiction, dance is the twists and turns of plot as the character endeavors to achieve a goal or solve a problem.

Doorway - The point in story where the protagonist chooses to step through a threshold in which there is no turning back.

Emotive - Highly emotional; capable of producing intense feelings.

Emotive Conflict - The character's emotions in conflict with what is happening in the story.

Exposition - Those items in narrative that the author includes to reveal information and description but does not move the story along.

Framing - Metaphorically to put a frame around a character, in which the story happenings reveal who the character is; a device to show rather than tell.

Internal Dialogue - The inner thoughts of a point of view character.

Motivation - That which propels a character into action.

Narrative summary - Summarization of what happened off-stage but is vital information for the reader.

Pace - The writer's ability to speed up action or slow it down to keep the reader engaged in story according to genre.

Plot - The story line. It is what a writer's story is about.

POV - Point of view refers to the character who is experiencing the scene with sensory perception. Writers are instructed to write the scene in the POV character who has the most to lose.

Premise - The "why" a writer is creating story. What is the moral truth to be explored?

Protagonist - The main character of a story who has a worthy goal.

Scene - The action portion of story, usually in dialogue, in which the POV character strives to achieve a goal, experiences conflict, and concludes with high stakes.

Sequel - The narrative portion following a scene with high stakes that contains a character's reaction, dilemma, and decision (to embark upon a goal).

Setting - Where a story takes place. It includes the where and when to introduce a psychological effect on the character.

Show don't tell - Allowing the reader to take part in the story progression with action instead of relaying what happened.

Style - The writer's unique way of presenting story.

Subtexting - Refers to the technique used in dialogue when a character says one thing but means something else.

Symbol - An item, usually tangible, that means something totally different through the eyes of the character.

Symbolism - The use of an item, usually tangible, to represent a particular meaning with emotive value.

Theme - The takeaway value of the story: how the story relates to the reader's life.

Villain - The character in story who opposes the protagonist; the bad guy who will stop at nothing to stop the protagonist. Every villain is an antagonist, but not every antagonist is a villain.

Voice - How a point of view character expresses herself in dialogue and inner dialogue.

Chapter 1 ~ The Beauty of Dance

To write is to feel the dance of your soul swirling in a dream
that drips imagination onto paper.
—DiAnn Mills

Rhythm, grace, and beauty describe a dance where two people move to music as though they were one. With perfect fluid motion, they sway and whirl, bend and lift—and we observe in awe. Simply by watching the couple express the joy of their unique gift, we are entertained, inspired, and encouraged to be better people.

Such is the art of writing a novel. The dance of character and plot blends unique steps that carry the reader away. The choreography varies with the genre, mood, and setting, as we will explore in the pages to come.

For the writer, this book will challenge you to reach your novel-writing goals, to learn the art of fiction, and apply those principles to your writing project. As a dancer must stretch before the music begins, the writer must stretch her mind to embrace the techniques of a master storyteller.

- Stretching requires determination.
- Stretching requires practice and application.
- Stretching requires scheduled time to study and write.
- Stretching requires discipline and commitment.
- Stretching requires writing when you don't feel like it.
- Stretching requires completing the exercises in these chapters.
- Stretching means you are on your way to success.

I've chosen an easy-to-understand method, using simple format and language. The stretching portion at the end of each chapter will help you apply new techniques to your novel. Learning these fiction skills is not difficult. Neither is the art a mystery, but it does take commitment to study and apply each chapter's information.

Our collaboration begins with this chapter and continues long after *The Dance of Character and Plot* concludes. For the new writer, the contents will help establish good habits—while adding new steps to your craft. For the seasoned writer, the reminders will help you tighten your manuscript. Writing quality fiction means a lifetime of learning and challenging ourselves. We must be limber, flexible, and open to change—while deeply appreciating what makes humans behave the way we do.

Professional Formatting

The basics of writing fiction begin by formatting our manuscript according to publisher guidelines. Adhere to one inch top and bottom margins and paragraph indents. Include a title page. Type the name of the manuscript and the contact information on the upper left. On the bottom left, type "copyright," the year, and your name. Insert a page break from your tool bar. Double-space your work and include a header, with your last name and the name of the writing project (Mills/Dance of Character and Plot). Leave room for the automatic page numbering. The header with the automatic page numbering begins on the second page. Do not use a footer.

Double-space the text of your story. Use a readable font such as 12-point Times New Roman or Courier. Fancy fonts and other deviations from publisher guidelines signify an amateur. You are a professional!

Don't depend solely on the submission guidelines posted by agents and publishers. Keep an up-to-date market guide on your shelf, such as *The Writer's Market,* published by Writer's Digest Books or *The Christian Writer's Market Guide,* compiled by Jerry B.

Jenkins and published by Tyndale. Market guides provide many opportunities to sell your work, connect with writers' groups, locate an agent, discover writers conferences, and even enter contests.

A tip: Before submitting a proposal or manuscript, email the literary agency or publishing house to ensure the agent or acquisition editor still holds that position. Verify the email address and the spelling of that person's name. Let's give agents and editors the respect they deserve.

Overcoming Your Excuses

A word about excuses. Sometimes it's hard to get started. We want to write, but we fear the hard work, so we keep thinking and talking about it—telling ourselves someday we'll write that novel.

Here are some common excuses for not writing. If one fits you, begin to stretch now to make amends.

Time

Establishing time to write takes discipline. Too often our schedules are like yappy dogs at our heels. Writing may mean getting up earlier. My alarm rings at 4:30 a.m. Yes, it's early, but it's also very quiet then. Your peak creative hours may come after everyone is in bed. Many writers have day jobs that include a lunch break. Brown-bag your meal and write. Motivation and a passion to communicate lead to scheduled writing time. As it's often been said, composing one page a day equals a book in one year.

Organization

Some of us are organized and others are challenged. If you struggle with this disorder, I'm sure you have a friend (opposites attract) who would love to help you get beyond the clutter. Treat her to lunch or offer to dedicate your first book to her.

Tools

A writer doesn't need the latest Mac or PC. Many published writers began writing on a computer at their local library. Harriet

Beecher Stowe wrote *Uncle Tom's Cabin* by firelight after she put her seven children to bed. I don't think she had an iPad. I wrote my first book in the second grade on a Big Chief pad with a #2 pencil. And an editor pored over this manuscript using a $300 netbook and a free, open source word-processing program.

Fear

Psychologists say fear of failure and fear of success rank the same on the stress scale. It can be scary to admit you're a writer. Enroll in a creative writing class, or submit your manuscript for publication. Tough it up. Write through the tears and conquer the shaky fingers.

Rejection

Rejection letters are redirection letters, nothing to be ashamed of. They are declining your material, not rejecting you. Usually you'll receive only a computer-generated letter. But if you're lucky, an agent or editor will take time to explain why the manuscript didn't fit their needs. Take encouragement from that personal attention. And keep submitting.

Writing is not for the weak hearted. It's a contact sport. Writers must be strong to finish the dance.

Maintain professionalism by reading current titles in the genre you want to write. Highlight passages that leap from the page. Study the authors you admire and respect. Read the bestsellers and dissect why the novel reached this status. Besides reading *Writer's Digest* each month, study how-to books and apply the principles to your work.

How are you holding up? Take a deep breath. Look how far you've come in the first chapter. The exercises in the next section, our stretching sessions, will help you apply what you've learned. When you are tempted to skip the exercises, remember when you stop stretching, your muscles stiffen. So stretch—and get ready for a dance that will never let you go!

Stretching

- Tell yourself every morning that you are a writer.
- Craft a mission statement. Include your passion for writing and your reason for penning a novel. Review it often.
- Make a list of your writing goals.
- Prepare a schedule for your writing. Stick to it.
- Write something every day.
- Get organized.

Chapter 2 ~ First Steps

To dance is to reach for a word that doesn't exist,
To sing the heart song of a thousand generations,
To feel the meaning of a moment in time.
——Beth Jones

Story ideas can be like fireworks. They soar and explode in beautiful colors…then their dance fizzles to the ground and we turn our attention to the next one. But story ideas don't have to fade away. A writer can take those wild moments of inspiration and build a credible, colorful, creative, and compelling story.

Where do story ideas come from? Everywhere! As Buzz Lightyear says, to infinity and beyond.

- Pieces of a conversation…juicy tidbits that move us to explore story and character
- An article in the news that grasps our attention
- Books we've read—fiction or non-fiction
- Music—including lyrics
- Poetry
- Nature—with all of its beauty and danger
- A movie you'd have written differently
- The behavior of family or friends
- Historic events about people and places
- Genealogy
- Personal experiences
- Dreams

Let's consider the topic of dreams. While some writers keep a journal of theirs, I'm not that systematic. But I've learned not to discount my dream world, which knows no time or place, where the impossible is probable. Deep within our subconscious activity lies this realm where plot problems find answers, character situations resolve, and new characters are born.

I remember a Christmas Eve dream when I was three. I'd gotten up to get a drink of orange juice. (My parents kept a small glass for me in the fridge.) I drank the juice and started back to bed, but first I wanted to peek out a window to see if Santa was close. And there he was! Riding across the sky! I hurried back to bed so Santa wouldn't skip my house. A dream? Maybe…but the next morning the glass was empty.

A few years ago, I dreamed about a mother with her two children exiting a mall during a downpour. She had her children sit on a bench beneath a covered pavilion while she hurried after the car. When she pulled around to pick up the children, they were gone. That became the story line for *Footsteps*.

I know you have a story idea. It's banging against your head and heart, keeping you awake at night. You're not sure what to do with all the information, and you fear you may lose it. So let's turn your burning thoughts into a book project.

Ready? Are your fingers poised on your keyboard? Our exercises will take a little time but are so worth the effort.

Step One

Write your story idea in one sentence. Don't concern yourself with character names, setting, and genre. That part will come in the following chapters.

A few examples:

1. A young mother confesses to her police officer husband that not only is she addicted to drugs, but she also deals them.

2. A businessman discovers the owner of his company is smuggling assault rifles into the country.

3. A newly married couple is left behind on a wagon train when the husband is suspected of carrying a terrible disease.

4. A young woman travels west to marry a man she's never met—only to discover he doesn't exist.

5. A diagnosis of Alzheimer's means a middle-aged woman must become the caretaker for her mother, with whom she already has a strained relationship.

6. A couple is wakened by thieves in their home. While the husband attempts to overpower the intruders, the wife is killed.

7. During wartime, a prince is forced to take the throne for his ailing father. Then the prince learns he's not the real heir, but the son of the warring king.

8. The people of a planet wracked by pollution face extinction. Their only solution is to exterminate half of the population.

Take a deep breath and congratulate yourself. You've given your story life.

Now perfect your one-sentence storyline. Tweak it until you're satisfied. Do you envision your protagonist(s) and antagonist(s)?

Some definitions may help:

Protagonist

The character who has a worthy goal to achieve or a problem to solve. Your champion, the character can be a hero or a heroine. A story with a romantic thread may have more than one protagonist.

Antagonist

Anyone or anything that stands in the way of the protagonist achieving her goal or solving her problem.

Villain

A character who will commit any deed to achieve a selfish goal. Every villain is an antagonist, but not every antagonist is a villain.

Step Two

Take your one-sentence idea and write at least one paragraph about your story. Extend the idea to include what you know about your characters and the storyline. (Close your eyes while you write this.) Don't worry about grammar and punctuation. Simply envision the story. When you're finished, save and edit your paragraph(s).

Step Three

What is your story's genre? Consider the list below and find a home for your idea.

1. Contemporary
2. Historical
3. Romance
4. Suspense/Thriller
5. Mystery
6. Western
7. Women's Fiction
8. Speculative (includes science fiction, fantasy, allegory, etc.)
9. Young Adult

Story ideas often mix genres with romance, such as:

Contemporary Romance

Historical Romance

Romantic Suspense

By including a thread of romance, writers increase their readership. It's been said that 80 percent of book buyers are women. Half of them buy romance. Do the math and consider adding a spark of love to your project.

Step Four

Where is your story set? Writers often view their story's setting as a character, sometimes as an antagonist. This helps build tension and conflict into your story. (We'll discuss antagonistic settings in chapter six.) By determining a time and place, you can establish the culture, vocabulary, and values of your characters.

Step Five

Establish your story's cast. List only those needed to carry your story idea to completion. (Limit the cast to twelve or less.) Give your characters names, but understand these may change once you dive into characterization.

On the left side of your screen, list each character's name. To the right, list the roles they play. Give characters multiple roles. Muddying the waters this way adds to the tension and conflict, building a complex story that resembles life.

Your cast will look something like this:

Character	Role
Mary	Heroine, who is trying to keep her flower shop from going bankrupt. She's in love with John.
Sally	John's sister. Her best friend is Jenny.
John	Hero, who wants to invest in Mary's flower shop to help her, but she refuses. He's in love with Mary but too shy to state his feelings.
Jenny	Mary's accountant and Sally's friend. Jenny wants the flower shop and is sabotaging the books. She's in love with John too.

Step Six

What do you want readers to learn from your story? Sometimes called takeaway value, this is your story's premise.

Dr. Stanley Williams has written an excellent book, *The Moral Premise*, about shaping this aspect. Williams opens the writer's mind to establishing the story's message throughout every scene.

A writer must have a reason to compose a story, a passion that carries through in everything the characters say, think, and do. The power of the premise lies in the characters' motivation to see their goal to the finish.

Take a deep breath. You've just completed the basics to writing your novel. Look at what you've accomplished and check off each item.

Stretching

- Write a one-sentence story concept.
- Write a paragraph (or more) about your story idea.
- Establish your genre.
- Establish a setting.
- Establish a cast of characters and roles.
- Establish the takeaway value/premise.

Chapter 3 ~ Breathing Life into Your Story

Fill your paper with the breathings of your heart.
—William Wordsworth

A dancer feels the movements, and her performance comes to life. She's passionate about her interpretation.

Think about the most memorable novel you've read. Did the story keep you awake long into the night as you clung to every word? What made the book grab you—and not let you go?

It was the characters.

A reader might not remember the plot, but those characters will live forever in her heart and mind.

Some writers believe plot trumps character. Others claim character is key. In my experience, characterization out dances any plot...but an outstanding plot will enhance characterization. So I suggest allowing character and plot to dance together, allowing each to complement the other.

Will you stick with a novel with weak characterization? One with a bad plot? What makes a novel stand out is the treatment of characters, and what makes the characters shine is the plot.

When we become immersed in a novel, we close the doors on the outside world until our beloved character solves her problem. We stay with the story because the writer breathed life into the pages by developing unforgettable characters.

I'd like to help you offer your readers the same satisfaction, for them to experience every step of your novel's journey through the eyes of a compelling character. And to leave them craving more.

Growing a Friendship

Consider your best friend. How long have you known her? I'd venture to say the process has taken years. Because writers don't have decades to detail one character, we need a way to speed the process. Your friend likely didn't burden you with her flaws at first. Instead she convinced you by words and actions that she'd be a great friend. The flaws came much later. By then you were invested in the friendship—and chose to overlook flaws because you cared. You became her cheerleader.

Backstory is the compass point to learning about your character. The crucial events and circumstances that motivate your character into spellbinding action become your goldmine.

> **Backstory:**
>
> **What happened to your point of view (POV) character before chapter one, line one, that influences who they are now? It's the foundation for behavior throughout your story.**

Handled well, backstory can be fresh, thrilling, and confidential. And for writers, as we learn a character's history, we find it easier to predict how they will act within the pages of our story.

People are four-part creatures who deal with the physical, spiritual, emotional, and mental realms. Our characters have the same challenges, and their backstory shows how and why they are motivated—to dance your novel's tango.

A character's responses may seem concocted—unless you have established through backstory why they behave as they do. The justification behind these reactions and relationships is best revealed through tiny nuggets seeded throughout the story.

✔ Backstory is your heroine's nightmare about the man who stalked her five years ago.

✔ Backstory is your hero's nightmare about how he drove recklessly and paralyzed his best friend.

✔ Backstory is your villain's nightmare about how his mother abused him, and now he preys on any woman with bleached blonde hair.

✔ Backstory is your heroine's cherished memory about her grandmother who encouraged her to sketch. Today she's a fashion designer.

✔ Backstory is your hero's fond memory about his dad receiving a medal for bravery. Now an adult, he's a police officer.

✔ Backstory is the villain's memory of the dog that listened to his cries when he was a little boy left alone by his mother.

Inside Their Heads

A writer cannot plunge protagonists and antagonists into action unless deep psychological needs are clear, and powerful, unresolved goals—both external and internal—are established.

How can you discover what these characters want and need, as well as their strengths and weaknesses? I've had great success using focused interview questions and personality tests.

A psychology book can offer substantial help to not only understand human development, but also to guide a character's behavior according to assigned traits. As a writer, you take the gathered information and observe the character reacting to the events of the story, guiding unpredictable yet realistic behavior. By discovering information about a character from every angle, you can create a picture of the character's life—physically and mentally—before the first sentence.

Believable character motivation is driven by emotion. A writer discovers why a character behaves a particular way by analyzing her backstory. This also helps you unveil her body language and internal dialogue. Is your character willing to make substantial sacrifices to reach her goal? Does she have mixed motives? Does she fight the truth behind her motives? You'll learn the answers in her backstory.

If she refuses to act, what are the consequences? A true hero or heroine always initiates action. He or she is never the victim, and the reasons lie in backstory. They may have been a victim in the past, but they vowed to never find themselves in that position again.

Robert McKee defines backstory best: "previous significant events in the lives of the character that the writer can reveal at critical moments to create turning points." In chapter seven, we'll discuss where backstory fits into plotting your story.

Inventory the character's childhood, then write about the experiences that formed her personality for the present story.

In her book *The Power of Body Language*, Tanya Reiman lists seven universal emotions:

Surprise

Fear

Anger

Sadness

Disgust

Happiness

Contempt

POV characters need to experience all these. Ask the hard questions your characters might not want to discuss. Force them to expose inner hurts and pain. In the depths of their forbidden and unchallenged world, you'll unearth the gems of temperament—and discover the power of motivation.

Perhaps your plotting and your story's opening lines will take a different twist. You never know where backstory may take you.

Stretching

(Inspired by *Writing the Breakout Novel Workbook*
by Donald Maass)

Consider who your protagonist is today:

- What events in her life up to age twelve affected who she is on chapter one, line one.
- What events in her life from age thirteen to twenty affected who she is today?
- What events in her life from age twenty-one to thirty affected her life?

Now consider recent events in your protagonist's life:

- What happened to her one year before the story opens?
- What happened to her six months before the story opens?
- What happened to her six weeks before the story opens?
- What happened to her twenty-four hours before the story opens?
- What happened to her one hour before the story opens?
- What happened to her ten minutes before the story opens?

More Stretching

- Complete each of the above exercises for your protagonist.
- Complete each of them for your antagonist.
- Now that you've answered those questions, how do you feel about your story?
- Has the opening or plot changed? How?

Chapter 4 ~ Characters with Personality

Character cannot be developed in ease and quiet. Only through experience of trial and suffering can the soul be strengthened, ambition inspired, and success achieved.
—Helen Keller

A dancer gives a spectacular performance, but only after years of sacrifice and sore muscles.

Now that you've established your backstory, you'll add another step by defining your characters. They evolve from a variety of places, then are shoved into a plot where they'll morph into even better characters.

We find our story's people in our friends and relatives, in dreams, in actors, in other books, in newsworthy persons, and from the eccentric creations in our mind. Drop them into a mixing bowl and flip the switch. The resulting blend sets the stage for a feverish dance of character and plot.

Every internal and external trait builds on the character's emotional being, which means everything about the character has the potential to influence motivation.

If a little girl has big ears and her mother insists she wear short hair, will the girl have confidence in her appearance? As an adult, how will those old tapes affect her as she repeatedly hears childhood taunts?

If a boy grows up without nurturing, how does he respond to potential relationships?

If a man raised in the heart of New York City is transferred to work on the Gulf in Louisiana, how will he adapt?

Ask Your Character Questions

You've begun to form an image of who your character is and what motivates her. It's time to use an online method of personality testing. I prefer Myers-Briggs (see http://humanmetrics.com). Through a list of yes and no questions, the test not only describes a distinct personality for your character, but it also gives vital information regarding habits and careers. It even lists famous people, real and fictitious, with the same personality. Once complete, the personality assessment will help you direct your character's behavior.

Personality assessments and psychology books do a great job of helping you understand your viewpoint character. But the more your write about her, the more of her character you reveal. Bland characters do not survive in the competitive world of publishing. Ours must be bigger than life—while living in a believable environment.

We learn characterization by doing. The stretching portion of this chapter will take you a little longer to complete, but your reward will be deeper insight into your character.

Stretching

- What is your character's name? Give her a name that reflects her role in the story. Other considerations are the story's genre, setting, and time period. Unusual spellings and pronunciations can confuse the reader, unless the distinction affects the storyline or characterization. I'll name our character Susan. Of Hebrew origin, it means "lily."

- What is Susan's age and birth date? Maturity is often a factor in stories. As we grow older, our values and opinions change, hopefully for the better.

- Does Susan have a nickname? What if her family call her Susie, but she despises it? How does her nickname affect her behavior?

- Birth order may indicate how a character views life, relates to others, and solves problems. What is Susan's birth order?

- Who are her siblings and how did she relate to them growing up? As an adult?

- What is Susan's personality type?

- What is Susan's height and weight? How does she feel about those markers?

- What is Susan's body build? What is her analysis of her body?

- What is Susan's racial or ethnic group? How does that affect her life?

- What are the size and shape of Susan's mouth, nose, and ears?

- What color are Susan's eyes? Do they have a distinct shape?

- What about the length and style of Susan's hair? Is she pleased with the look?

- How is Susan's health? Is she plagued with any medical conditions?

- Does Susan use distinguishing gestures or mannerisms?

- Where did Susan receive her education? How much education does she have? How does she feel about this area of her life?

- What is Susan's occupation and income? Is she satisfied with her lifestyle?

- Does Susan have a hobby or special skill? What is it? How much time does she devote to this pastime?

- Does Susan have a favorite food or restaurant?

- Is food important to Susan?

- Does Susan own a pet? What kind?

- Does Susan have any religious affiliation? What kind? If so, how important is faith to her?

- Is Susan experiencing spiritual turmoil?

- What is Susan's speaking style?

- Does Susan have a sense of humor?

- How does Susan approach friendships?

- Does Susan have a best friend? Close friends?

- How does Susan feel about her family? How does her family view her?

- What is Susan's social status? Does it matter to her? Does she want to change that aspect?

- Who does Susan admire? Why?

These questions will enable you to know your character. Her answers will help you create someone well-rounded and believable, yet capable of surprising the reader. Every characteristic has the potential to affect the character's psychological development.

More Stretching

These questions will help you establish credible motivation by understanding Susan's emotions.

1. What makes Susan angry? How does she display her anger?

2. What is Susan's most painful experience? Elaborate.

3. What are Susan's political and social views? Is she radical?

4. What are Susan's fears? Mental or emotional problems? Describe.

5. What scenarios embarrass Susan?

6. What does Susan appreciate about life?

7. What does Susan despise about life? What would she do to change those things?

8.   Who would Susan like to be? Why?

9.   What have you learned about Susan? List three to five main strengths, weaknesses, wants, and needs.

10.   What is Susan's external problem? Does she know how it could be solved?

11.   What is Susan's main inner problem? Does she know how it could be solved?

12.   What is Susan's goal? What would she do—or not do—to achieve it?

Take a deep breath. Now review your answers. Are they consistent? Do you like this character? If she is a villain, do you understand how and why she makes bad decisions?

Don't stop now! Continue to spend time with your character. Ask questions—and wait for answers. Next we'll go a step deeper and discuss more of the psychological aspects of character.

Chapter 5 ~ Deepening Characterization

Heart is what drives us and determines our fate. That is what I need for my characters in my books: a passionate heart. I need mavericks, dissidents, adventurers, outsiders, and rebels, who ask questions, bend the rules, and take risks.
—Isabel Allende

Two dancers fall. One gets up and tries again. The second hobbles off. A dancer who believes in her art knows that a fall means she is a step closer to success.

We just discussed the foundation for developing memorable characters. We learned how interview questions can help us assign physical attributes and explore basic motivation. Now we'll dive deeper into the inner landscape of characterization and increase our understanding of the psychological workings that fuel motivation—and how to surprise readers with behavior that's in character.

Learning the inner qualities of characterization takes time. Personality testing establishes if a person is an introvert or an extrovert. Introverts tend to do better reading others' emotions. Extroverts are easier to read.

Out of character comes plot, which means the writer determines those qualities that motivate a character to act. She has a problem to solve or a goal to achieve, and the story begins. By posing critical questions to a character, you as the writer can discover dark secrets, hidden ambitions, fears, dreams, hopes, and desires. The answers reveal what topics to include in the plot—those the character desperately wants to avoid. By being forced to attempt what she fears, the character changes and grows.

Sometimes a character changes for the worse, especially an antagonist.

Sometimes a character doesn't change, especially in a series where the character's behavior works for the story line. James Bond has all the skills needed to overcome the bad guys. Indiana Jones possesses what's needed, no matter the situation.

The psychology of a character allows a story to progress, because the writer must keep raising the stakes, either physical or internal. And readers become involved in the character's life and care what happens.

Essential Needs

All people are created with three distinct needs:

Relationships

Significance

Security

By Any Means

Some devices a flawed character may use
to fulfill his or her three basic needs

- **Money.** Do finances rule your character's thoughts?
- **Power.** Will your character do anything to obtain control?
- **Sex.** To what length will your character go for intimacy?
- **Possessions.** Does the desire for material things drive your character's actions?
- **Appreciation of beauty.** Does your character have a soft spot for any of the arts that distracts and weakens her?

According to the Bible, these needs were designed to be filled by an intimate relationship with God. But thanks to Adam and Eve and their taste for fruit, we were pitched out of the garden. Stubbornly, we try to find our own way. Understanding our character's weaknesses avoids marionette characters who simply arrive on a scene and await someone to pull their strings.

Your character also has unmet needs vital to her well-being. Even if legitimate, the motivation to satisfy them may result in poor choices.

A need to survive

Is your character—or someone she loves—threatened? Is she driven by obtaining food, clothing, or shelter?

A need to feel financially secure

What will your character do to pay the bills?

A need to feel emotionally safe

Does your character have unresolved issues that drive her behavior?

A need for intimacy

Does a need for friendships and sexual relationships cause your character to take foolish risks? How far will she go to feel accepted?

A need for significance

What will your character do to feel important? Are her self-esteem, competence, and independence threatened?

A need to fulfill goals

Will your character be tempted to make poor choices when her goals seem too difficult to achieve?

A need for an identity

Will your character be assertive to live up to her uniqueness? Will she make mistakes that cost her everything?

Determining if your character makes decisions independently or as a member of a group will also help you identify those areas of her life that are in good order—and those that need strengthening. Independent behavior can be noble, if a character takes a stand for a worthwhile cause. But if the results are self-serving, an independent stand can be selfish. Likewise an action based on the good of the group can be admirable, as when members of a business team cooperate. But in the context of a dysfunctional group, poor decisions can follow, as when a gang leader convinces members that a wrong is right.

Writers who form a complex character and environment can create unpredictable behavior—responses that are true to a personality but not foreseen. Many heroes and heroines are not aware of their admirable qualities until they are forced into an intense situation.

Every character in a novel is dealing with a disruption, crisis, or problem that forces her out of her comfort zone. A strong, well-developed character realizes her past coping mechanisms can no longer handle the situation. New skills are needed. To succeed, she has no choice but to accept the difficult task.

As your novel progresses, the character may not realize the slip in her dance step. But by the end of the book, she will not only realize her error, but will also have made major strides to improve her quality of life. Your responsibility as the writer is to determine if the character has the courage, determination, and openness to accept the challenge.

Nancy Kress in *Dynamic Characters*
suggests a four-part dynamic for creating
convincing character change

Preparation	showing the character has the capacity for change
Pressure	the events that challenge emotional equilibrium
Change	the actual moments of change from where the character began
Validation	demonstrating the character has truly changed

Character is developed through adversity, which gives your protagonist hope that life is worth living and worth living to the fullest. In turn your reader finds hope in her own circumstances—and is encouraged to make needed changes.

A further reality of writing fiction: if you do not see a transformation in your own life as you write, then you have failed. If you cannot see the premise of your story fulfilled, how can you expect a character and a reader to step forward with new optimism?

Stretching

- Does your character see herself as an independent thinker—or does her identity come from a group?

- Does your character view her goals as an expression of self—or does she rely on the group?

- What matters to your character: her self-expression or her responsibilities to a group?

- When your character is challenged, does she seek to make changes—or look to a group for solutions?

- Does your character define her own morals or does she look to a group's values?

- Does your character have many relationships or few? Why?

- Does your character gauge her behavior by her unique personality or the guidelines of a group?

Chapter 6 ~ The Dynamics of Setting

*Remember in your story that setting is the other
character. It is as important to your story as the people
in it because it gives them context and can ideally be used
to heighten drama and tension, depending on where it is.*
—Rob Parnel

No matter where a dancer performs, the setting is as much a part of her gift to the audience as her leaps.

In this chapter we'll dive into the depths of setting and its importance to story. Too often writers ignore setting or give it a minor role—instead of exploring the power of where a scene takes place. Establishing a unique setting takes skill. But once mastered, it gives your story a new dimension.

Usually setting is physical, but it can be mental as in a dream world, an unconscious state, or hallucinations. Whatever the location, setting can keep your characters—and the plot—moving in directions that aren't always obvious to the reader. When a surprise occurs in setting, it should be seamless. The character's response to an unexpected change in her environment keeps the reader turning pages.

Research forms the core of a setting's credibility. How far will you go to ensure your story is factual? What will you do so your manuscript can soar with authenticity? Are you ready to step outside the boundaries of your comfort zone? This often means traveling to the setting and exploring where your character experienced life. Only when a writer is prepared to conduct research beyond the minimum will readers find reason to applaud.

We've briefly talked about using setting as an antagonist, which increases the stress, tension, and conflict on the protagonist striving to achieve a goal. To ensure a tight, high-stakes scene, use the character's fears and weaknesses against her. This forces the character not only to struggle, but also to face an inner and outer antagonist: fear and setting.

What aspect of setting tips the scales toward the antagonist? Outline those characteristics of an unexpected force rising against the protagonist—and watch plot twists emerge that can take the story deeper.

Setting has its own characterization sketch. Establish the time, date, season, and the culture where your story takes place. You can reveal aspects of the settings in characterization, plot, dialogue, and narration—and use it to evoke symbolism and emotion. Treat setting as something vital and full of spirit. The more real you can make the setting, the more muscle you add to your story, because it forces your character to respond.

Make sure the setting works against the protagonist. The adversity can be obvious or hidden, but include ways that pressure your character into making tough decisions, then accepting responsibility for them. Always challenge your character to leave her comfort zone.

As an example of an antagonistic setting, consider a protagonist who has a beautiful garden surrounded by a ten-foot stone fence. The garden is her source of tranquility, and she spends hours in the garden. But one day a villain follows and traps her inside. Her peaceful domain becomes her torture chamber.

Why make life easy for your protagonist? Seek ways to ensure she changes and grows throughout the novel by facing one difficult situation after another.

A wise writer shows enough setting for the reader to envision the story world—and no more. Information overload cheats the reader. If you reveal too much, the reader will skip the description and move on to the action—at the risk of missing an important detail. Allow your reader to experience the same thrill as your character feels as she journeys through the setting.

A character who lives in the setting will not make the same observations as one who is a visitor. The seasoned character will respond differently than a novice. For example, a veteran police officer understands the challenges of her job better than a rookie, who is either nervous or overconfident.

Research

Accurate research focuses on sensory perception. Consider not only what a character would see and hear, but also what she would taste, smell, touch, and intuitively sense. During a research visit, take lots of notes and photos. Bring along a recorder for interviews with people who live there.

In your note-taking, consider the seven universal emotions (see chapter three). Use active verbs and strong nouns to show how your character's qualities can give your story additional depth.

What you see in your research takes many different facets. Seeing physically means recording all those details that impress you about the setting—yet knowing only one or two items will be all you'll need. But sight is not limited to the physical realm. Consider what's in your mind's eye. A writer's imagination weaves what she sees with how she will use the information.

For a historical story, imagine the details of yesterday and blend them with what you see today to paint a word picture of the setting and its people.

Logic is another part of viewing the setting. Will the information you gather build realism? What have you discovered that brings a fresh touch to your story?

Have you looked, really looked, at the people you interview? What does their body language reveal as they speak about special moments? Painful moments? People remember events according to their own sensory experience. These memories can add a personal touch or help you sort out truth and logic.

What do you hear when you conduct your research? Some years ago, my son and I visited Gettysburg. We were so moved, we thought we heard the cries of the soldiers. Listen to the sounds of nature. Tune your ear to the dialect of those you interview.

Understand the culture, the unique vocabulary, the subtleties, the laughter, and tears.

A great way to communicate local flavor is by evoking the sense of taste. Whether you are in the States or halfway around the world, depicting food and drink brings a richness to your writing. Ever watch a travel show? By showing a restaurant, a food vendor, or a meal in someone's home, you can offer insight into that culture.

Dig into the traditions and customs for the setting's smell, whether offensive or enjoyable. As you step into that other world, you'll find sensory ways to draw readers into the world of your story.

This means brushing your finger across the vegetation, dipping your feet into the water, petting an animal, or embracing someone different. Experience the surroundings. Pick up a baby or hold a hand. Laugh. Cry. Ask questions. Touch pulls us into someone else's world. This may be difficult, but it always brings a reward.

Ideally to receive the total sensory spectrum, a writer should visit her story's setting. But that is not always possible. If you use a real place, be sensitive to those living in the community. Research cities, streets, and businesses or use fictitious names to avoid offending residents.

Libraries hold a wealth of information. Websites offer much, but make sure your online research is verified in at least three places before putting it in print. Pick up the phone and call the area. The chamber of commerce often has more information on a subject than any website. Churches, diners, museums, libraries, newspapers, and historical societies are rich sources of information.

True research into your story's setting means investing to benefit others. Your readers deserve to experience the adventure of your writing. Ensure your manuscript includes sufficient depth of detail to touch hearts and lives.

Setting and Genre

Each genre uses setting to give the plot definition. The genre's specific traits provide a means to expand premise, theme, character growth, and symbolism.

Consider these scenarios:

Romance

When a tropical storm threatens the safety of young lovers, a Caribbean island that once looked idyllic—with sun-kissed days on white-sand beaches and nights filled with the perfume of exotic flowers—turns into a nightmare.

Fantasy

In a kingdom far away a benevolent monarch is deposed by a tyrant who places a heavy burden on his subjects.

Historical

Breathtaking mountain peaks become deadly after a wagon train attempts to cross them too late in the year. Then the lure of owning property in the west is countered as a cattle baron threatens new settlers.

Science-Fiction

An isolated, peaceful planet is invaded by aliens who require the inhabitant's life source.

Contemporary

A rural community known for its charm and family appeal is hit by a mile-wide tornado.

Suspense

A pleasant city known for its many churches is plagued by a series of unexplained bombings.

No matter your genre, take time to brainstorm your story world. Use your imagination. Study the settings of your favorite writers to see how they make them pivotal to their stories. Then list ways your setting can be exceptional.

I hope your mind is spinning with possibilities of how to make setting play an active role in your story—and provide an exciting stage for your characters.

We may be able to visit the settings for fantasy, science fiction, and some historical fiction only through the portals of our minds, forcing us to rely on other forms than hands-on research. Below you'll find ways to help make your setting come alive.

Stretching

- Visit the area's chamber of commerce.

- Conduct a web search of the area. Some apps will help you with this: Google Maps, Google Earth, Weather Bug, or travel sites that can be found via apps or websites.

- Take or download more pictures than you think you'll ever use.

- Interview people living in the area. For a historical setting, this also means reading diaries and journals. How has history affected the community?

- Listen to how local people talk. Do they use a distinct vocabulary?

Ask questions about your setting:

- What are the community's values and expectations for life and each other?

- What is their diet? How much of their food supply is local?

- How is the area governed?

- What are the local hotels? Restaurants? What's featured on the menus? Any daily specials?

- What are the sources of entertainment?

- How do the people celebrate holidays?

- Does the community have special festivals?

- How does the area experience the seasons, and what are average temperatures?

- What are the medical concerns? What kind of medical care is available?

- In what kinds of homes do the people live?

- Where do the people shop?

- How do the people dress?

- Do the arts play a vital role in the community?

- How do the people view education, sports teams, and favorite colleges?

- How do the people earn a living?

Other Considerations

- If the area is near a national or state park, look for research material in the visitors section.

- Discover the wildlife and birds of the region.

- Locate a map of the area.

- Visit the local library. View newspaper archives.

- Look for documentaries on the area.

More Stretching

List your character's fears and weaknesses. Now incorporate them into setting. Compose several paragraphs in which your setting acts against the character and forces her to deal with those shortcomings.

Do you include scenes where you place your character in unfamiliar territory? If not, how can you add or revise setting to raise the stakes for your character?

Chapter 7 ~ Plots That Dance, Part I

*Once you have invented a character with three dimensions and a voice,
you begin to realize that some of the things you'd like him to do
to further your plot are things that such a person wouldn't or couldn't do.*
—Thomas Perry

We all want our novels to dance. Our characters are authentic, fascinating, and irresistible. We're researched our setting so thoroughly, we know the area inch by inch. But if our novel lacks a substantial plot, our story will never receive an invitation to join the dance of a publisher's list of new releases. In this chapter we'll begin to explore effective plotting.

Our plot is the story idea. How will a character reach her goal—and change along the way? Will that story dance with readers?

The first line of your novel plunges the reader into your story world. I like what Donald Newlove says in *Painted Paragraphs* about the hook sentence. "It is about the white-hot opening whose glow speaks for a story's greatest strength: its spirit."

The hook is an emotional invitation. The writer issues a subtle promise that every word will be as powerful as the opening line. And she spends hours honoring her commitment. Take a few minutes to read the hooks of some of your favorite novels. How did the hook raise a question that caused you to continue reading?

Superb novels require two essentials: strong characterization and an exceptional plot. They go hand in hand, an organic cultivating of suspense as a highly developed character accepts the story's challenge.

☞ Some writers claim to outline their entire novel
before beginning the story.

☞ Some writers claim to fly by the fingers of creativity.

☞ Some writers believe novels are plot-driven.

☞ Some writers believe story is all about character.

☞ Some writers use a mix of what works best for them.

You've probably figured where I stand on those issues. No matter what philosophy you choose, a few facts inspire all writers. Motivation draws characters into facing their opposition by expertly weaving stress, tension, and conflict into every scene. Your protagonist strives to achieve an impossible goal. Stumbling blocks escalate, and the antagonist appears to be winning. All seems lost for the protagonist, but in the process she has undergone a dramatic transformation. The final battle, then victory! (Yet a few series heroes, like Indiana Jones and James Bond, seldom change. They simply use their skills to solve problems.) Antagonists ultimately face the consequences of their actions, possibly growing worse in the process. No wonder readers keep turning pages.

Remember our character Susan? Let's toss her into an uncomfortable setting and see what happens.

Stress

Susan checked her lipstick one more time before exiting her car. A cacophony blared from inside the town hall, electric guitars and drums that reminded her of a war dance. Actually it was. She could do this. Spend the night listening to music and watching him, her favorite dancer. Across the parking lot a local TV station crew carried in equipment.

She shoved a twenty inside her jeans pocket along with her car key and hurried inside. The town hall nearly burst with people, laughter rising above the music. Scary. Her stomach churned at the thought of someone speaking to her. But she managed to slip into a corner…and wait.

That, my friend, is stress. Note that Susan is attending the dance alone. The idea of seeing her dance idol is enough to make her leave her comfort zone

Tension

A hush fell over the crowd, and those in the middle of the dance floor squeezed back. He'd arrived. Now he would select a partner from the adoring women vying for his attention. Susan couldn't see him, but his choice of a partner wasn't why she'd come. Simply watching him dance would fulfill her dreams.

The crowd parted, and he strode toward Susan. She sensed the blood drain from her face. A camera man followed, filming his every move.

"I choose you," he whispered, and took her hand.

"But I can't dance." Regret seared her stomach.

"That's what they all say." His smile set her quivering. He pulled her to the dance floor. The crowd cheered, a deafening roar in Susan's ears.

She tried to escape, but he held her hand with a powerful grip.

A heavy dose of tension. Susan's emotions are taking a beating. How can she save herself?

Conflict

The lights flash on in a whoosh. The lead singer calls out a beat. The TV camera focuses on her, and the lights are blinding.

"I don't know how to dance." Surely he'd understand and stop this madness.

He draws her into his arms. The music begins. Her knees shake. The dancer smiles. "Don't make me look bad."

Three steps into the music, and Susan tramples his toes. She mumbles an apology. The idea of stumbling over his feet for the entire song makes her ill.

He scowls. "You'll pay for this."

Susan tries to twist from his hold. "I told you I couldn't dance."

He tightens his grip.

"No one threatens me," she says. "I'm calling security."

And the conflict…well, you decide.

Conflict results from characters struggling to achieve their wants and needs. It involves inner and outer battles, and your book must have both. Susan wrestled with shyness while attempting to communicate that she didn't know how to dance. Desire ruled her actions and thoughts.

Combine desires with strengths, values, and flaws—and the writer has complex characters who react and initiate the story's conflict. How these characters try to resolve strife reveals who they are. We had no idea that Susan practiced maintaining healthy boundaries until the dancer burst into her personal space. The element of surprise showed that she would not take his threats lightly.

In everyday life, we try to avoid conflict. It's frustrating, it interferes with our plans, and it complicates life. But we must have it in our stories.

Conflict can be:

- ✔ with another person
- ✔ with nature
- ✔ physical
- ✔ mental
- ✔ spiritual

In a novel, the conflict must be so compelling, the reader notes the stakes—and a high risk of failure. Force your readers to engage with the character's emotions—drive her car into a raging tornado or down an icy mountain slope. Shock her. Terrify her. Make her laugh and cry. Give her a time limit with heart-wrenching consequences, and stack the odds against her. Reward her victory, then plunge her into another conflict that shows that reaching the goal is inconceivable. Draw out every possible emotion.

Inner conflict needs to be equally strong. The issues can be mental, emotional, or spiritual. Often these are problems the characters don't want others to know about or deny their existence. These psychological issues are critical in the black moment.

Inner conflict reveals your character's motivation. In a romance, a hero's goal may be to win a particular girl. His outer conflict is that he can't ask her out because she has a boyfriend. But his inner conflict may be a terrible fear of rejection because his parents are highly critical.

Every page of the story must have some type of stress that leads to conflict; the reaction and response must contain strong emotions. (We will explore the power of explosive emotive conflict in chapter ten.) Your character has been thrust into a difficult situation, and the story is about her reaching deep inside to overcome the obstacles aligned against her.

Scenes and Sequels

Story is made up of scenes and sequels. Sometimes this is referred to as action/reaction or cause/effect. Scenes are the action spots, usually containing dialogue.

These questions, given to me by a copy editor at Tyndale House Publishers, are essential to writing tight scenes.

1. What is the POV character's goal or problem?

2. What does the POV character learn that she didn't know before?

3. What backstory is revealed? (Refrain from inserting backstory in the first fifty pages other than a phrase or a teaser that raises curiosity.)

4. How are the stakes raised for the POV character?

Every scene has a viewpoint character stepping into action with a goal, a conflict, and a disaster. A disaster doesn't have to be earth-shattering, but something that stops the character from achieving her goal and raises the stakes. Scene is written in short, fast-paced sentences. This is also a crucial spot to deepen characterization by showing how the character faces adversity.

One's character deepens when faced with challenges. We learn to trust—or not to trust—a situation according to the protagonist's responses. Everything she does to improve her situation actually makes things worse.

A sequel is the POV character's internal response to what just happened, commonly called exposition or narrative summary. This is also called the reaction or effect portion.

The sequel is the "catch your breath" moment. It allows the viewpoint character to work through what just happened. In today's novels, this may be merely a single line or phrase of inner dialogue. It's a pondering of her dilemma, making a decision, and going forward with a new plan or goal. The dilemma and decision portion may even be assumed, and the character simply chooses to move forward. Often there are two or three scenes before a sequel.

New writers often make the mistake of overwriting sequel. Keep this section clear and concise, with emotion that equals the intensity of the scene.

When tempted to overwrite, consider where your eyes go on the written page. Do you tend to skip over slow, lengthy paragraphs and move your eyes ahead to the white space—dialogue, where the action happens?

Do we want our readers to be skippers? Or do we want them not to miss a single word?

Susan, a police officer, races down the expressway after a suspect. She increases her speed. The perp weaves in and out of traffic, and Susan continues her pursuit. Her squad car swerves out of control. She is powerless to stop the skid, and her car crashes into an embankment.

The writer has given Susan a goal, a conflict, and a disaster. The sequel to this scene would not be:

- I should have picked up my dry cleaning.
- I forgot to complete yesterday's paperwork.
- Did I remember to put on deodorant this morning?

Absolutely not! The sequel would most likely be: Susan screamed and slammed on the brakes. In that short sentence, she experienced a reaction, a dilemma, and a decision.

In the next chapter we'll explore the ingredients for an irresistible beginning, a gripping middle, and a dramatic ending. Until then, keep practicing those dance steps!

Stretching

1. What is your protagonist's goal in the story?
2. What is your antagonist's goal?
3. Write an opening hook. Does it pose a question or arouse curiosity?
4. Write your story's first scene by using the plot questions.

Remember the four questions for each scene:

1. What is the POV character's goal or problem?

2. What does the POV character learn that she didn't know before?

3. What backstory is revealed?

4. How are the stakes raised?

Chapter 8 ~ Plots That Dance, Part II

Plot is no more than footprints left in the snow after your characters have run by on their way to incredible destinations.
—Ray Bradbury

A choreographer blends steps, motion, and form into an emotionally unified interpretation that flows with music. The art of writing novels also combines intricate techniques that raise and diminish action and blend it with emotion.

In the previous chapter, we considered how careful plotting is crucial. We discussed the importance of a strong hook, various kinds of conflict, and scene construction.

Now we'll focus on what goes into your novel's beginning, middle, and ending. This is not formulaic writing, but a guide to writing a novel filled with tension and conflict in just the right places.

So how does the writer know what constitutes her novel's beginning, middle, and ending? Read on.

Beginning

The first approximately one quarter of your novel is the most crucial. In it you must form a sympathetic bond between the protagonist and the reader, introduce other characters, and unfold plot—while building conflict and suspense. Too much exposition and a reader loses interest.

These elements will help you build a strong beginning.

✔ A strong hook that draws the reader into the story. Open in the middle of action. This taste of the conflict to come promises that the four-hundred-page dance will be filled with adventure.

✔ A unique, sympathetic character who endears the reader to the story.

✔ A story disturbance. This is not the story problem, but a frustrating intrusion into the protagonist's life. How the character responds creates a bond with the reader, who becomes the character's cheerleader.

✔ Strong characterization of the viewpoint protagonist—and antagonist. These characters must come alive. And the antagonist must be better equipped to succeed than the protagonist.

✔ A problem to solve. This can be something to achieve or overcome.

✔ Stress, tension, and conflict that lead to suspense. A writer establishes these essentials by continuously placing trouble in the character's path. One way to initiate action is through dialogue in which the characters are at odds. We'll examine this technique in chapters eleven and twelve.

Also:

Establish the novel's genre: contemporary, historical, romance, suspense, fantasy, science fiction, thriller, western, young adult, or any of the other genre. Romance is often paired with other genres.

Plan the setting, ensuring it is vital to your plot.

After encountering these elements in the first quarter of your story, your protagonist decides to go after the goal. She steps through the first doorway into the plot with a firm resolve to do everything within her power to succeed, including adding to her arsenal of resources.

Middle

Here is where a story can weaken and fall apart. In our dance of character and plot, sometimes the storyline drags. But this doesn't happen if we carefully plot this section and include subplots with exciting twists and turns.

Consider your character's traits and the current problem. List the worst possible scenarios. Make a what-if list for all the viewpoint characters. Be creative. You'll discard some of the ideas—and use others to create an intricate plot.

Study the character's psychological traits. Your best scenes will happen when a character behaves the opposite of what the reader expects. But your reader will accept those unexpected actions because you've demonstrated the character is not predictable. Suspenseful conflict is achieved with scenes that cast doubt on the protagonist achieving her goal. The antagonist always has a bigger dance team and better choreographers. And she's willing to do anything to stop the protagonist.

Heightened tension keeps the reader turning pages. Give the reader a moment to take a gasp of air, then drop her back into the action.

Every plot idea you can muster has already been written. Multiple times. From the ancient storytellers who gathered around the campfire, to Greek and Roman mythology, to the richness of the Celts, to the many ways story is offered today. Every culture has personalization. Take a look at the many TV series introduced each season. Within the first preview, you can recognize a basic plot.

Dr. Dennis E. Hensley of Taylor University offers examples of the nine basic plots

Character vs. character

Cowboys vs. Indians

Yankees vs. Rebels

Cattlemen vs. sheepherders

Character vs. himself/herself
Silent Snow, Secret Snow by Conrad Aiken
High Noon (staring Gary Cooper)

Character vs. God (or the gods)
Job—Old Testament

Character vs. the machine (technology)
2001: A Space Odyssey by Arthur C. Clark
John Henry vs. the steam drill

Character vs. society/culture
The Great Gatsby by F. Scott Fitzgerald
Downton Abbey

Character vs. the unknown
D.O.A. (starring Dennis Quaid and Meg Ryan)

Character vs. setting/environment
Earthquake
Armageddon
The Day After
Twister

Character vs. situation/circumstance
The Poseidon Adventure
Towering Inferno

Character vs. fate/destiny
Oedipus Rex

Don't put a bombproof shield around your character. Let her face the consequences of her actions—no matter how disastrous. Pit her against insurmountable odds, descending into an abyss where we'd never venture.

Why were we drawn to Indiana Jones and his adventures? The writer used Indy's fear of snakes to add to his likability. And his rugged good looks caused women to envy the actress opposite him—and men to wish they could accomplish his feats. We were glued to our seats. As it should be.

Subplots

Take advantage of the middle as an opportunity to include subplots.

- Problems involving minor characters who have valid issues
- Something about a viewpoint character that is separate from the main story idea

These subplots add tension and conflict as they weave another level into your story. The mini story lines force more turmoil into your viewpoint character's life, ushering in emotions that can rip her raw. But she deals with these difficulties and moves on.

The wrap-up to subplots occurs when the main story climaxes and a resolution is established. Will your character reach her goal? Can she be successful when the antagonist is making sure the odds are against her? Keep the reader guessing.

While using surprise and unpredictability, don't deceive your readers. Understand the varying degrees of point of view. (More on this in chapter nine.) If Susan is going to freak out when a dog follows her around the block, you must already have given the reader some hint of her fear and its cause. Use a sprinkling of foreshadowing and backstory to make it believable.

Complications

I suggest you throw a huge, heavy wrench into the middle of your story. What can happen that will seriously affect the plot and the characters' lives? This could be:

- ✔ new information
- ✔ unexpected complications

- ✔ eliminating a character
- ✔ changing the setting

A "whoa, I didn't see that coming" scene foils readers who think they can read the beginning of a novel then skip to the climax and resolution. A damage-inducing plot twist provides reader satisfaction, which ripples to more readers for your next novel… and the next.

Sol Stein suggests raising the stakes by giving characters opposing scripts. In other words, two characters have different agendas. They enter a scene with their own goals in mind—and miscommunication sizzles. Try this and watch the sparks fly.

Building Credibility

The writer's mission is to make the seemingly impossible occur in such a way that's believable. The *Spider-Man* movie offers an example of how an incredible comic book hero can be made to look realistic by establishing him as a sympathetic character. He has real problems, inner and outer, that produce incredible conflict. An ordinary young man is bitten by a radioactive spider. The spider bite gives him the ability to accomplish heroic feats. But what about his inner problem: the girl next door? We stay with him from beginning to end.

Do you remember *Star Wars*? How many of us have walked into an airport and thought how the people resembled the characters in the cantina scene? That's conflict in the making!

Choices and Doubts

The middle is also where the protagonist realizes her struggle to reach her goal is taking a lot of work. Doubts set in. Have you ever given up? Decided a goal wasn't worth the trouble? Considered quitting? Maybe we gave up for a while. We want our characters to mirror our emotions, and we want them to overcome their fears to succeed.

Consider the choices confronting your character. Have her choose between two rights. Which one? Why?

Looking for still more conflict? Force your character to choose between two wrongs. Imagine the guilt, the responsibility, the consequences, and the circumstances surrounding her dilemma. Make her life messy, with the storyline and characters believable, but also bigger than life.

Chapter hooks, especially through the middle, are as vital to your story as the hook at the beginning. End each scene with high stakes, an outer or inner struggle that spins with emotion. You'll keep the reader up all night turning page after page to discover what happens next.

Other Techniques

Flashbacks can be tricky, and I suggest avoiding them. But if your story cannot be told without one, transition in, construct the flashback scene filled with action, and quickly transition out. Stay in deep point of view (see chapter nine) and limit use of "had." Introduce the transition with the past tense "had," then refrain from using it for the remainder of the flashback.

In his book *Fiction Attack!* James Scott Bell recommends avoiding flashbacks for the first fifty pages. My opinion? I'd rather gain ten pounds than deliberate if a flashback is critical to my story.

Another plotting technique you may consider is a façade story. According to Donald Maass, a façade story presents as true certain information that's later revealed as false. For instance a character believes something and projects that to the reader, who has no reason to doubt because the reader trusts the character. As the story builds through one suspenseful scene after another, the character learns she's been deceived. The new information ushers an unexpected dimension into the resolution.

The movie *High Crimes* uses this technique. A man is arrested for murdering innocent people while serving in the military. His wife, a lawyer, believes him and risks her life to prove his innocence. But after he's exonerated, she discovers her husband is guilty. The movies *Sixth Sense* and *Secondhand Lions* are also façade stories.

Caught in the Crucible

Sol Stein suggest using the "crucible" as a means to drive the plot forward. He defines it as an environment, either mental or physical, that bonds people together. The crucible is greater than their desires, and neither is willing to give it up.

As an example, Stein cites *Moby Dick*. Neither Captain Ahab nor the whale will give up the sea.

Consider a married couple with two children who have drifted from their relationship. Both husband and wife have a significant other. Yet neither one wants a divorce because of the crucible—their children. Or consider the situation in a lifeboat. Which passenger wants to give up her seat?

Resolution

The latter portion of the middle is where the climax occurs. A torch ignites the inevitable. It's catastrophe time. Whatever has been crucial to the protagonist has been destroyed. The real character—the inner landscape character—must solve the insurmountable problem.

In a sense, the protagonist is naked. All she has to help her is what she's learned on the journey. Every possible emotion must play before the reader through action—spine-tingling, heart-wrenching action. The dance of character and plot spins out of control.

The resolution serves as the reader's moment to relax and appreciate the protagonist's ability to beat the overwhelming odds. All significant loose ends must be tied—including solving the secondary characters' problems. Still, there are times when minor occurrences or unadjusted personality traits are left to the reader's imagination.

Craft an ending that will satisfy. Avoid a jolt of the unexpected and unbelievable. The reader has committed to a dance, and the writer can't leave her standing alone at the end of the song.

This plotting graph will help you see
where to place the beginning, middle,
and ending items of your story.

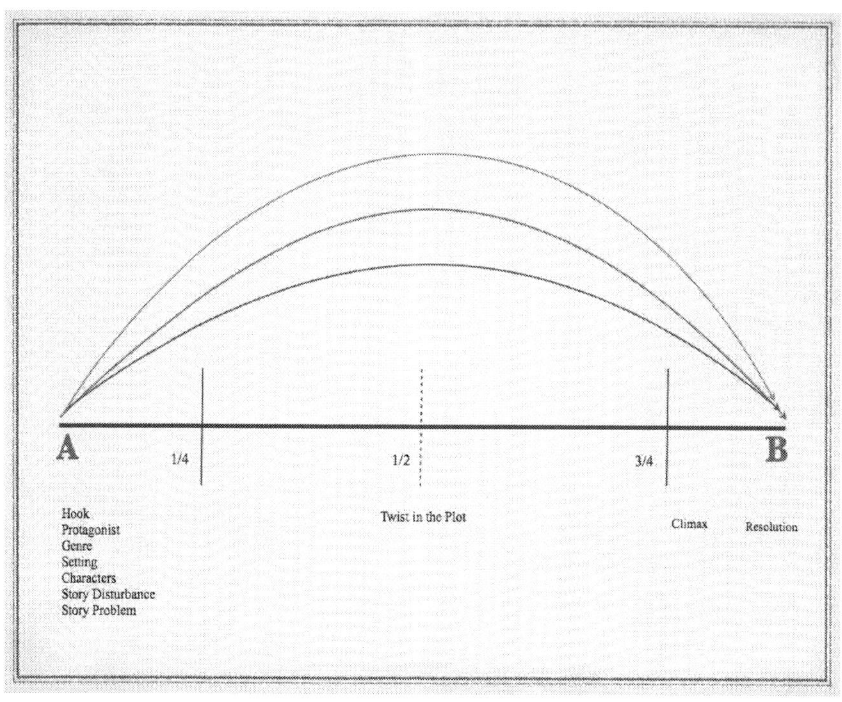

Stretching

- Examine your novel's beginning. Have you established the necessary criteria by the first doorway?

- In the middle, what event changes everything? How does this affect the character reaching her goal?

- Consider the resolution. Does this last section fit the character's goal and the story's theme? Have you tied up all the loose ends? Did you choose to leave something for the reader's imagination?

- Write a scene with these elements:

  > A man and a woman have been dating for over a year. She is certain he will propose this Saturday night, during their dinner date at an exclusive restaurant. He loves the woman, but he's not ready to propose. On Friday morning, he is invited to go hunting for the weekend. He makes arrangements to meet her for lunch. She thinks he can't wait to propose, but he wants to convince her he should go hunting.

Chapter 9 ~ Point of View

You never really understand a person
until you consider things from his point of view.
—Harper Lee

The lead dancer takes center stage. All the others complement what she's doing and may even exit for her spotlight. There's no doubt who the audience is supposed to watch. Point of view is as easy as picking out the star dancer.

- "Whose head are we in?"
- "Which character sees and internalizes every aspect of the scene?"

Have you ever been asked these questions? Critique partners, agents, editors, and readers demand to know—from the first sentence—the scene's viewpoint character. This character is the one experiencing the scene, and we want the reader to vicariously live the adventure with her. Our character cannot read others' minds, she can only assume from what is said, from evaluating past information, or by guessing from body language.

A writer scratches her head and studies the proposed story's characters, conflict, and plot. How do you choose POV? Are there guidelines?

The viewpoint does matter. It affects the scene, with its potential tension and conflict, and ultimately the story.

In the planning state, a writer has two aspects of POV to determine:

- What type of POV?

- How many POV characters are needed for the story?

Let's take a few moments to discuss first, third, and omniscient POV. I don't recommend second person, in which the writer invites the reader to be the "you." This POV can be accusing and turn the reader away from the story. While second person may work for a few nonfiction projects, it tends to fall flat in fiction.

First-person POV

Everything is told from the narrator's viewpoint of "I." The advantage is intimacy. It's easy to believe what the character says, thinks, does, and experiences—similar to a friend telling you about an event. Or like reading a diary.

First-person POV is frequently used in literary and mainstream novels but also in detective stories. To the reader, the writer takes on a dual role of character and author, thus increasing emotion right from the beginning. The reader cares.

The disadvantage comes from interjecting the writer's thoughts and feelings instead of using the character's traits. Another problem is describing the character without sounding self-centered. A third problem is perspective. The first-person narrator may have unreliable information. Will the reader feel cheated or deceived when her treasured character is proven wrong?

A writer can use a single first-person POV or multiples. If using multiples, identify the viewpoint character's name before the scene or chapter begins.

As with all other POVs, with first-person you'll use only one character's viewpoint per scene so the reader stays engaged and not confused.

Third person POV

In third-person, you'll use "he," "she," or the character's name.

First-person:	I hurried to my car before the rain soaked me.
Third-person:	She hurried to her car before the rain soaked her.
First-person:	"Please, just one more chance?" I needed this job to survive.
Third-person:	"Please, just one more chance?" She needed the job to survive.

Third-person is the most popular among writers. Multiple third-person POVs gives the writer a variety of perspectives from which to show the story. When using multiples, identify the character in the first sentence of each new scene or chapter.

Omniscient POV

Omniscient point of view means the writer can inhabit several characters' heads at the same time. But this makes it difficult for the reader to form a bond with a single character. The story may appear distant and confusing, and the reader may not understand why. Omniscient viewpoint leaves little room for the reader to find a wisp of mystery. This was a common technique in classic literature, but today's readers prefer to be part of the adventure by experiencing a single character, one scene at a time.

Point of View Levels

Varying degrees of point of view allow you to set the amount of psychic distance between the reader and the character. According to the goal of the scene and the character's temperament and role in the story, you can choose in third-person to write distant, close, or deep point of view. Powerful scenes emerge from deep point of view, but I've also read terrifying scenes from a distant viewpoint.

Deep point of view allows the reader to easily step into the viewpoint character's shoes, experiencing every action and reaction through the character's senses. What appeals to you more: a movie on TV or a 3-D experience? This is what deep point of view accomplishes. But not every movie is best viewed in 3-D. Examine your point of view characters to see if they're a candidate for deep point of view.

If you wish to master this technique, search for areas in your manuscript where the character sees, hears, tastes, smells, or touches—and rewrite the passage so the character experiences the action. Key words to avoid are realized, wondered, scanned. Often telling prepositional phrases can toss the reader out of the character's head.

Go Deep

Distant: She heard the crack of thunder.

Deep: The thunder startled her.

Distant: He scanned the workers laboring over their computers until he saw her blonde head.

Deep: Her blonde head stood out against a room of African-Americans.

Distant: She stared at him in disgust.

Deep: She wrinkled her nose.

Deep point of view helps you to show rather than tell, but the technique is more about creating a close bond between the character and reader. The internal dialogue, emotions, and body language must come from the character's heart and mind, providing the reader with an intimate experience.

Choosing POV

In selecting POV you must establish what characters are needed to accomplish the novel's theme and purpose. In the chapters on plotting, we discussed the need for the main character to achieve a goal or solve a problem. The fewer the viewpoint characters, the tighter and more focused the story. Every time a reader has to change POVs, a shift occurs and she must make an adjustment.

So how many POV shifts are needed to show your story, while still keeping your reader engaged? A tough decision!

In *Writing the Breakout Novel,* Donald Maass suggests listing the characters needed to show your story. Limit the list to less than twelve. Beside each character's name, assign the role she will play. Study your list. Where can a character play more than one role? Can she play three?

Giving a character more than one role muddies the waters—making life difficult for the protagonist and sometimes the antagonist. The higher the stakes, the more a character will risk to reach her goal.

Multiple viewpoints can add depth to your story. Think about a huge family celebration. What dynamics have the potential to ruin the event? You want to invite Uncle Jake and Aunt Sally, but he picks fights with anyone who disagrees with his obnoxious declarations about other family members, politics, religion, and a list of topics. Aunt Sally attempts to calm him, but it's useless. Their children are bullies and always in trouble. Still, Aunt Sally is a sweet lady, you don't often see her, and her health is failing. That's life—and your story.

How does you choose the best character viewpoint for the scene? Ask two questions:

- Who has the most to lose in the scene (highest stakes)?
- What role will this character play at the climax?

Sometimes a story calls for an unreliable POV. This could be a character who is biased, possibly a liar, mentally or emotionally unstable, or someone simply too close to a situation. This can be effective in a story where miscommunication fuels the conflict, such as a romance or a suspense novel that portrays a villain's POV. An unreliable character acts according to the truth as she sees it. Remember if you choose an unreliable protagonist, your reader has to connect with her early on and care—at the cost of being deceived.

Challenges arise in choosing to place POV with problematic characters. If you give the perspective of a child, make sure the language reflects the age and culture, as well as the child's emotional, mental, spiritual, and physical attributes. Other challenges come with:

A character who is hearing impaired.

A character who is speech impaired.

A character who has lived in seclusion.

POV determines your novel's language, setting, and atmosphere. That character is the focus of your reader's attention, so for the full dramatic effect, you need to keep her on stage. Keep the scenes tight and full of suspense, but make sure she's dancing long enough for readers to understand the goal, conflict, and high stakes.

Go ahead. Select the perfect viewpoint(s) for your novel.

Stretching

Write a scene based on one of these scenarios. Choose the point of view from the character who has the most to lose.

The setting is a bank where a robbery is about to take place.

✔ Character A is the robber. He's lost his job and is about to have his home and his car repossessed. There's no food in the house, and his wife plans to leave tonight with their two children if he doesn't bring the cash to buy groceries.

✔ Character B is a police officer. His entire life is wrapped up in his career. A month ago, he was diagnosed with stage 4 cancer. He's determined to leave his family a heroic legacy.

✔ Character C is a bank teller. She's a single mother with two small children and doesn't receive child support. Recently she was reprimanded for the number of errors in her drawer. If it doesn't balance today, she'll lose her job.

✔ Character D is a contractor. He has to make a deposit before noon or he'll bounce several thousand dollars from employees' paychecks. An alcoholic, he needs a drink badly. He's nervous, irritable, and fearful of losing everything. A week ago he learned his only son was killed in Afghanistan.

There is no right or wrong answer. Just choose the best viewpoint character for your story line.

Point of view changes everything about your story.

Chapter 10 ~ The Dynamics of Emotion

He liked to observe emotions; they were like red lanterns strung along the dark unknown of another's personality, marking vulnerable points.
—Ayn Rand

The lure of dance lies in the passion of the performance. Caught up in the excitement, we forget the outside world. Our hearts are swept away in a flurry of unexplainable, captivating feelings. Emotion…the soul of any art.

Passionate involvement is why writers write—and readers turn pages.

Along our journey, I've emphasized creating conflicting emotions. In this chapter, we'll discuss how you can master this technique. You'll learn how incorporating powerful feelings can make the difference between rejection and acceptance.

Do you ever wonder how to fill every page, paragraph, line, and word with the same mojo your favorite author uses? Writers look for the magical ingredients to craft a page-turning, energetic, bring-me-more novel. Our goal is to carry our readers firmly into our story world.

Whether you're an aspiring new writer or a veteran, this chapter will help you add suspense through emotion.

Fixing Flats

A few years ago, I attended a Donald Maass workshop on writing powerful emotions. At a low point in my career, I wanted to get out of the game, but my stubbornness wouldn't let me. My manuscript was flat, and I couldn't figure out how to fix it.

Maass' teachings and his book *The Fire in Fiction* changed the way I create story. I learned how to feel my character's actions and reactions—and why readers value the passion of emotion. Since that epiphany, I've earned numerous awards. Pick up Maass' book and absorb every word.

Readers are passionate about experiencing story through the eyes of the character. They want to live each moment: the good, the bad, and the terrifying. Communicating characters' feelings adds an emotional charge to any novel. That requires not simply filling the pages with the character's emotions, but communicating the feelings of characters in conflict:

"I love you, but I hate you. Seeing you with another woman proved how much you don't care."

"I'm depressed because I've been fired. But I'm glad I don't work for that jerk anymore."

"I want to move to the country, but I don't want to leave my friends."

"I want to join the Marines and defend my country, but I'm afraid of getting hurt."

Get the picture? Characters dealing with conflicting emotions sparks our readers' attention.

While on vacation in the Big Bend area of West Texas, my husband and I stayed at a lovely but remote resort. Because of the distance to the next town, the employees lived in staff housing. I met a beautiful Korean girl who had contracted to work there for a year—and had two weeks before she could return home. We talked about missing family, friends, home…and at the same time we said, "And Starbucks." Although from different parts of the world, we each were strongly drawn there.

Getting to Know You

Writing explosive emotions begins with knowing our characters. This means concentrated work to establishing the character's:

✔ temperament

✔ wants

✔ needs

✔ goals

✔ strengths

✔ weaknesses

It's impossible to write how a character feels unless you grasp her personality.

Whatever your method of characterization, it's most important to knowing your character's psychological makeup. Use whatever method works best for you to understand what drives your character into action.

Making Connection

Readers and characters connect when the character experiences honest feelings and the reader responds with her own.

✔ "Oh, I like you."

✔ "Your heartbreak makes me cry."

✔ "I'd be angry too."

✔ "You can do it!"

I recently spoke with a friend who hadn't slept the previous night. At three in the morning, she decided to pray for everyone in her life. After several minutes, she realized she was praying for the characters in one of my novels. What a huge compliment! She'd become emotionally attached to my characters!

Additional Hooks

It's not enough to include a strong hook in your novel's first sentence—or even the first sentence of each chapter. Also include a hook in the last line of each scene. This creates a need for the reader to continue. The hook can take the form of an unanswered question or an unresolved action. Exceptional hooks create emotive conflict within the point of view character—and the reader.

"You don't know her secret," Win said to me. (*Long Lost* by Harlan Coben)

A moment before the encounter, a strange expectancy overcame Grady Adams, a sense that he and Merlin were not alone." (*Breathless* by Dean Koontz)

When I wake up, the other side of the bed is cold." (*Hunger Games* by Suzanne Collins)

We had been wandering for so long I forgot what it was like to live within walls or sleep through the night. (The *Dovekeepers* by Alice Hoffman)

I, Guinevere, Celtic Princess of Rheged and only child of King Leodegrance, woke to a clatter of activity in the stableyard. (*Child of the Northern Springs* by Persia Woolley)

None of us needs to be writing a story about which we don't feel passion. If we're not excited about the characters and their problems, how can we expect a reader to stay with them for four hundred pages?

The emotion in a scene must match the story's tension and conflict. If there's too much, the scene is overdone. If too little, the scene falls flat. The bigger the action that prompted the reaction, the more intense the response. Writers use the what-if technique to brainstorm the worst thing that could happen to their character. This means the character must endure heart-wrenching emotions.

Using Your Pain

To write a successful novel, we must confront our own feelings. Our mission is to transfer gut-reactions into the lives of characters. This requires getting in touch with our feelings, past and present. Writers who refuse to identify their own responses to life can't effectively write emotive conflict. If we deny our own pain, how can we convey the pain of our characters? Readers can spot counterfeits.

This exercise, from *Writing the Breakout Novel Workbook* by Donald Maass, is one of my favorites because it takes the writer into the memory and emotions that underlie behavior. Take the exercise seriously and it will deepen character motivation—and make the scene worthy of publication.

What is your most painful experience?

Jot down a few specifics: setting, date, sensory perception, and those who were present.

Place your character into the same situation, using all the emotions you identified in your own painful moment.

I presented this challenge at a writer's workshop, and one woman claimed she couldn't record her most painful experience. Too difficult. I suggested she complete the exercise when she returned home. Eighteen months later, at a conference awards banquet, a publishing house presented that writer with her first book contract. Afterward as I worked my way through the crowd, she called my name. She was crying. She said she'd accepted my challenge and incorporated her most painful experience into the life of her character in the opening chapter. The editor told her that after reading that scene, she had to publish the book.

Be willing to write honest emotions. Imagine your character standing before a firing squad. But the shooters are firing one at a time—and the character is allowed to duck. Sometimes she's wounded and sometimes she successfully dodges the bullet, but each time she learns another strategy until she eludes the final shooter.

This illustrates not only how emotive conflict should dance through your novel, but it also provides insight into your theme and premise.

When you write with emotion, you invite your reader to be part of the story.

James Scott Bell in *Revisions and Self-Editing for Publication* says this: "To show character emotion in such instances, look to action, metaphors, and dialogue."

This means the story spins away from the telling zone and solidly into showing.

Spectrum of Symbolism

Various symbolism techniques also effect emotion, especially color.

Red is a warm color that engages strong feelings, from warm and comforting to angry and hostile. Experts claim red can stimulate the appetite. What color is your kitchen? How do these phrases affect you: redneck, red-hot, red-handed, paint the town red, or seeing red?

Blue prompts a range of psychological responses from calmness to serenity. Studies show workers in offices painted blue are more productive. Blue can help a dieter keep her weight in check. But blue can also mean sadness. Anyone enjoy the blues? Blue Monday? When was the last time you had a blue ribbon day?

Green, which symbolizes nature and growth, has a calming effect. Have you ever taken a green plant to an invalid? It's been shown that people who work in offices painted green have fewer stomach aches. Green can also signify wealth, greed, or jealousy. In the fifteenth century, when green represented fertility, wedding gowns were green. Think about that the next time you select a green M&M. How do these phrases affect you: green thumb, green with envy, greenhorn?

Yellow is often described as cheery and warm, but it can also be a color of frustration. More tempers are lost in yellow rooms, and babies in yellow rooms tend to cry more. The color can also stimulate the appetite. What about the coward who's called yellow?

Or a yellow traffic light? Do you want to be known as Miss Sunshine?

Purple is the color of royalty, wealth, wisdom, and spirituality. It can also mean arrogance, magic, or mystery. Experts find that children like purple, a mixture of red (passion) and blue (calmness). How does your character feel about purple?

Brown invokes a down to earth feeling. Farmer Brown and Farmer Green were neighbors. But for a person who feels isolated on a farm, brown can symbolize sadness.

Pink is a romance color: loving, feminine, calming, and soothing. Many book covers for romance novels contain a shade of pink. Consider the phrase "in the pink" or the color of Pepto Bismol.

Orange, a mixture of red and yellow, means excitement and enthusiasm. It's also associated with autumn, the end of the growing season and the entrance into winter.

White signifies purity and innocence. It can also represent spaciousness or sterility. How can you include white to create emotion in your character?

Black can mean evil, power, death, and mourning. In the fashion world, it's used to create a slimming effect, even sophistication. Consider these phrases: Black Death, blackout, black cat, black list, black market, black tie, black belt.

Gray, a blend of black and white, often symbolizes life and death. A gray sky can bring much-needed rain for thirsty crops. But a gray sky that turns menacing can usher in floods, and a gray-green sky may signal a tornado and danger.

Sounds of Emotion

Word choices can also reflect emotions. The sounds of a character's words can influence mood and setting.

Hard consonants create a feeling of harshness. Brisk. Terse. Cut. Kill. Dank.

Many words that end with "y" are light, even fun. Pretty. Dainty. Lovely. Perky.

Words that roll around in the mouth are fun to write, and we don't have to be Mary Poppins fans to appreciate supercalifragilisticexpialidocious.

Words with soft consonants are soothing. Add a long vowel sound and we can relax our reader's heart rate: Oh, honey.

Writers of romance use words and phrases expressing beauty, love, and longing that reveal the character's feelings.

The rhythm of our sentences can also underscore emotions. Writers who read their work aloud or use text-to-voice software hear how their work sounds. If a passage seems harsh when you meant to create a calm scene, or if a sentence contains a poetic lilt when you wanted to show violence, revise your phrasing.

Using Body Language

Body language and emotions are dancing partners. A character can deny how she feels, but her body language will give her away. *The Emotion Thesaurus: A Writer's Guide to Character Expression* by Angela Ackerman and Becca Puglisi is essential for every writer. The book pairs emotion with body language to help writers create realistic responses. Earlier we talked about Tonya Reiman's *The Power of Body Language* and the seven universal emotions: surprise, fear, anger, sadness, disgust, happiness, and contempt. I use both books to avoid trite responses.

If a writer wants to expand her knowledge of human emotions, explore these twenty-four feelings:

anxious

angry

happy

hopeful

panicky

sad

hurt

helpless

bored

annoyed

regretful

relaxed

envious

depressed

tense

jealous

cynical

caring

confused

impatient

joyous

guilty

excited

serene

Yes, exploring these emotions is a challenge, but a writer who strives to show credible behavior will write quality fiction. Our heroes and heroines are not perfect, and once the character has befriended the reader, emotions affect the relationship.

When you hit a roadblock in conveying emotion through dialogue, reach into your memories for a highly emotional time. What was said? Do the words still echo? The words a character says with the deepest emotion are the ones a reader remembers. "Frankly Scarlett. I don't give...."

In her book *Dialogue,* Gloria Kempton says angry people don't make sense. How true. The tirade can continue for years. We don't need to compose line after line of useless dialogue, but we can show a character out of control. This is another area where you can search your experiences.

The masterful writer can twist the heart of her character—and her reader. This works for any genre. Think through

Showing Feelings

Show your characters' feelings in thought, word, and body language. Avoid stating the feeling: "I was sad." Instead write creatively to show what the character experiences.

The thickening in my throat stopped me from speaking. I sank into the chair and buried my face in my hands.

"What's wrong?" he said.

I pointed to my phone. "There's a message from the Coast Guard."

My sister's eyes filled with tears. "Dad's boat?"

I reached for her hand. "Empty."

history when passionate writing moved people to accomplish great or infamous things. Words can build up or destroy. Consider a time in your own life when words encouraged or defeated you.

Seize heart-wrenching moments. Be honest with your character's feelings. Be bold. Raw. Rip open scars. Then stand back and admire the best scenes you've ever written. Just keep a box of tissues beside your keyboard.

Emotive conflict. Where will it take you?

Stretching

Consider times you experienced the seven universal emotions. What prompted those feelings? Record the who, what, where, when, and why—as well as the intensity.

> Surprise
>
> Fear
>
> Anger
>
> Sadness
>
> Disgust
>
> Happiness
>
> Contempt

Now look at your expanded list of emotions. How does your character express those feelings?

More Stretching

How does your character show anger? Study your character's personality, backstory, and assigned traits. Be specific with an element of surprise.

Now compose a scene in which your character reacts with anger. Are you pleased with the results?

Chapter 11 ~ Writing Dialogue that Sparkles, Part I

I've found that good dialogue tells you not only what people are saying or how they're communicating, but it tells you a great deal—by dialect and tone, content and circumstances—about the quality of the character.
—O. Wilson

A dancer's steps are not choreographed merely to take up space on a stage or fill in the bars of a score of music. They have purpose: to deepen the meaning of the performance.

Readers devour dialogue. They want to hear what characters have to say and how they say it. They want to learn about the problems, the plot, and all the exciting happenings of the characters' lives.

Dialogue written just to take up word count wastes the writer's talent and the reader's time. Dialogue is able to accomplish so much more. Good dialogue is fresh, exciting, and oozes with potential conflict.

I like to think of dialogue as a war zone. When a writer declares war between characters, the page becomes a battlefield, and the verbal and nonverbal exchange explodes on your manuscript.

"Kim, isn't it your turn to clean up the kitchen?"
"Yeah, Dad, I'm on it."
"That's what you said thirty minutes ago."
"It'll get done."
"Now."
"Hey, I'm busy."

"You're texting. Now."

"Get off my case. You aren't even my real dad."

"Hand over your phone and your car keys."

"That car's mine. You have no right to—"

"I bought it. It's mine."

Read a passage of dialogue from one of your favorite authors. Note the crisp word choices and the rhythm of the spoken word. Some fiction experts claim dialogue's purpose is to move the story along or enhance characterization, but I prefer what Gloria Kempton says: "Dialogue's purpose, and there is no exception to this, is to create tension in the present and build suspense for what's to come…Effective dialogue always, always delivers tension."

If a passage you've written doesn't fit that description, hit the delete key or rework the scene. The verbal exchange within your story must stay focused—which is not what happens in real conversations. So how do we create dialogue that sizzles while ensuring it sounds real?

Begin with characterization: knowing the characters' personality and their wants and needs. This allows their words to be authentic. It also takes time: pages of writing drafts of scenes to discover the character and watch her in action. This means only one character can say a given line. Never cut and paste dialogue from one character to another. Interchangeable lines signifies mere talking heads, with no individual word choice or defining actions. Taking shortcuts means the writing suffers.

Have your character speak as soon as possible. Get her involved in a conversation with another character—someone who challenges her, disagrees with her, frightens her, loves her. The way a character handles confrontation helps a reader to identify with her—and begin to form that crucial sympathetic bond. A reader judges who the character is by how she handles trouble. Expertly written dialogue shows the character in situations she wants to avoid—and we are eager to read that response.

Establish a vocabulary for the character and stick with it (unless there is a distinct reason to change it). Always think word choice and the reader's ability to understand what the character is communicating.

Before I begin a novel, I write pages of backstory. I want a document of what's gone on in the life of my viewpoint character before page one. This allows me to deepen characterization, weave a tighter plot, and compose focused dialogue.

When you discover what motivates your character—and why—her problems and goals become more evident. The character has unresolved issues and is preoccupied with them. That motivation shows up in her actions and what she thinks and says.

Ever have a conversation with a three-year-old who wants a cookie? The child will say or do anything to convince you she needs a cookie.

"Mommy, can I have a cookie?

"It's too close to dinner."

"Please."

"No honey. You can have a cookie after your eat your meat and vegetables."

"But I want it now."

"After dinner."

"You look pretty today."

"Thank you, but no cookie."

"I still be hungry for dinner. I promise."

"Wonderful."

"I pick up my toys."

"Okay, here's your cookie."

"Can I have one for each hand?"

Make sure your dialogue contains conflict—even between characters who normally agree. No conflict; no reader satisfaction.

Dialogue means more than words. Silence is also an effective tool. Use body language—in the form of action tags—to relate what the character truly feels.

With a good understanding of body language, you can compose effective dialogue using nonverbal communication that demonstrates emotion, even when the character doesn't realize what she's revealing. Communications experts say up to 90 percent of communication is nonverbal. Including body language enables you to show and not tell.

Envision each scene—perhaps even act it out. Put yourself in place of the character and let creativity take over. Have conversations with the characters and place them in varied settings. See how they respond. The adventure begins when the character opens her mouth and steps on stage. Study screenplays and the art of screenplay writing, where dialogue carries the plot.

When witty and fresh dialogue pushes the plot toward the finish line, the reader will want to pick up the writer's next book—and the next.

Stretching

Compose a line of dialogue for each POV character in your story. Use language only that viewpoint character would say—but no speaker tags. Show your work to someone who knows your story to see if she can identify who is speaking.

Select a passage of dialogue from your story. Remove all the descriptions and action tags. Do the words alone still convey the correct meaning?

More Stretching

Use this scenario, selecting one of the characters listed. Write a short scene, using dialogue, in deep point of view.

A man leaves work late and hurries to his vehicle. His son's soccer game starts in ten minutes, and he promised the boy he'd be there. The man feels a tug on his arm. He swings around and realizes two teenage boys are trying to snatch his wallet.

The man is:

- An off-duty cop
- A lawyer
- A pastor
- In the middle of a panic attack
- Working for organized crime

Chapter 12 ~ Writing Dialogue That Sparkles, Part II

*It made me alive to the fact that the most important thing sometimes
is what isn't said—to prepare for moments of revelation that can
be read entirely on actor's faces without dialogue.*
—Robert Towne

The time comes when every dancer realizes her skills have to strengthen if she's going to reach her goals. Her practice hours increase. She searches for a coach who can challenge her. Her performance must match what her heart is telling her.

In the previous chapter we discussed the basics of writing dialogue. Now we'll explore how a writer can use dialogue to create tension and conflict.

Successful dialogue focuses on warfare, both verbal and nonverbal exchanges. This is the life and breath of every novel.

Gloria Kempton says dialogue can be indirect, subtle, and ambiguous.

Thomas Sawyer says dialogue should be tight, realistic, original, unexpected, authentic, and rhythmic.

Those are tough measuring sticks!

Consider your character's dialogue. Is she always direct? Or is she ever ambiguous? Does what she says raise questions? Does she pose situations that leave others confused? Frustrated? Speechless? Do you use subtexting to add another layer of meaning to the passage? If your characters are accomplishing those, you are well on your way to dancing with dialogue.

Here is a passage from my novel *Breach of Trust*. The hero, a high school football coach and teacher, has brought a student to the public library to find a book for a report.

Miles leaned onto the desk top. "I have no idea, but I'll find out. Any help you could throw his way will be greatly appreciated." He couldn't even tend to business with Paige without his blood pressure rising to the point of needing medication.

"We've got a couple of books here about Jim Thorpe. I can find more info online. I'll pull something together before you leave."

"Thanks. I read in the paper that Daniel Keary donated the new computers."

A cold stare replaced the warm glow. "What of it?"

The sudden shift of mood caught Miles off-guard until he remembered the phone call he'd overheard when she'd told someone to "pick them up."

"So you're not overly pleased about Daniel Keary's generous contribution?"

Paige smirked. "Don't look a gift horse in the mouth. But that doesn't apply to Trojan horses." She took a stack of books from a small boy and touched his cheek.

Miles studied Paige until the little boy said his goodbyes. "Obviously, you haven't jumped on the bandwagon to support Keary."

"Has it started to snow in July?"

"But he's conservative, stands for pro-life, wants to lower taxes, and he's a Christian. I read that he's served his country well, too. The other guys are jokes."

"Even Lucifer was called 'Morning Star, Son of Dawn.' Don't be suckered by the image, Coach."

"Hey, you know something I don't? He looks like a shoo-in."

"Whatever. You can nominate him for sainthood. I'm sure his office can supply the forms."

Miles was taken aback by her sarcasm. The woman he'd grown to know had never been vicious before. "Give me one plank of his platform that you disagree with. That's all I ask."

"You're right. Keary stands for good things. He's against abortion, lowering taxes, and supports faith-based initiatives, but a woman has a right to her own opinion."

"What is it that you dislike about this guy?"

Paige pulled a book from the shelf. "He shouldn't have had to give back his medals."

"Keary?"

"No," Paige said, walking away. "Jim Thorpe."

Writing in-character dialogue means being true to the story's premise and theme while creating scenes that lead to the climax. One of the writer's considerations is composing dialogue appropriate to the genre.

Fantasy

Fantasy writers can invent words to make their imaginary setting a place of beauty and mystery. Fantasy story world is reflected in a culture that is predominantly medieval, reaching into Celtic, Greek, and Roman folklore, legends, and mythology. Magic often plays a role in the plot. Dialogue can be poetic, and even sound romantic. But beware of using too much archaic language and syntax. Just as you can hint at a dialect without going overboard with creative spelling, a few well-chosen phrases can allow readers to hear the fantasy world's speech. Creating a glossary at the beginning of your novel helps the reader visualize and experience the fantasy story world's culture.

Romance

Romance writers can use poetic, flowery language to show how a relationship develops with a happily-ever-after ending. Characters see the world in unexpected beauty, and unlikely characters can be humorous or giddy. (A romantic element can be woven through every genre.)

Horror

Horror writers use dark words and hard consonants to frighten their characters and readers. Symbolism also plays a role in producing fear, whether real or imagined. Horror, says Clive Barker, "shows us that the control we believe we have is purely illusory, and that every moment, we teeter on chaos and oblivion."

Suspense

Suspense writers want to snag the reader's breath. The characters are surprised, verbally or physically attacked, or sense something is about to happen. So the writer uses words that indicate anxiety or unpredictability while the character attempts to discover the truth or stop an event with disastrous potential.

Historical

Historical writers use era and setting to play a vital role in showing how events occurred, plus the when, where, why, and goal of the story. Through the important tool of language, convey culture and values, while painting a credible depiction of the times. For *11/22/63*, Stephen King used the slang and attitudes of the late 1950s and early 1960s with great effect.

Contemporary

Writers keep up to date on language, technology, setting, and all the nuances that shape a contemporary character. Stories set after World War II are generally considered contemporary, but if you're going back more than ten years, expect to research that year's phrases, entertainment, and controversies. Remember how in the first *Back to the Future* film, Marty McFly found himself lost in the world of his parents' youth? We'd be just as challenged to fit into the world of 1985, when the film was made.

Contemporary Young Adult

Writers of contemporary young adult understand youth are immature and inexperienced. The dialogue is raw, edgy, honest, and lacks subtlety. If you have experience with a teenager, you know what I mean.

Below the Surface

Dialogue that says what the character means—and nothing more—cheats the story and the reader. As Francine Prose says, "Dialogue usually contains as much or even more subtext than it does text. More is going on under the surface than on it. One mark of badly written dialogue is that it is only doing one thing, at most, at once."

That's when you need to reach for the technique called subtexting. In the previous chapter, we talked about body language that spoke louder than the character's words. Subtexting concerns the real conversation going on between the lines of the spoken dialogue, the highly charged thoughts and feelings that characters don't express directly. Use this technique at every opportunity.

Subtexting is especially important when characters who dislike each other are forced to communicate, work together, or live where they must get along. People aren't always completely honest with themselves, or others, which sets the stage for ambiguity—and conflict.

Try these tips to help you compose dialogue that sparkles.

- Select word choices and gestures that establish the speaker.
- State an occurrence once. Show the response—but not what was stated. The reader will understand without repetition.
- Avoid using italics for a character's thoughts. Each time italics appear, the reader must make an adjustment, which throws the reader out of the story. Also italics are more difficult to read in e-books.
- The best dialogue happens when two people enter a scene with different goals. She wants to find out if he really loves her, but he wants to see if he can break their movie date so he can go hunting.
- Avoid repeating first names: "Marsha." "John." "Marsha." "John." A pronoun is more intimate.
- Avoid having the character spell things out. RTUTE: resist the urge to explain. Dialogue meant to show a writer's research distracts from the story.
- Always be listening: in restaurants, at family dinners, in crowds. Keep a notebook and jot unique dialogue.
- Be willing to condense and be concise. Avoid adverbs.
- Use only "said" as a dialogue tag. Any other word, even "asked," calls attention to itself. The syntax and the question mark makes it clear to the reader.

- Avoid semicolons. Except for professors and politicians, we speak in phrases or short sentences.
- Limit exclamation points. Use word choice, body language, and the mood to convey the tone. Stronger language allows the reader to feel a part of the experience more than a punctuation mark. In the dialogue below, it's clear, without special punctuation, that Susan is fleeing for her life.

> "A man is after me with a knife." Susan raced through the crowd.

Punctuation in dialogue can be a problem, but a review of an English grammar guide will help.

Here are a few common problem areas and solutions.

End punctuation is placed inside the quotation marks.
"I want to read a novel."

Use a comma before the quotations marks if a tag is used.
"I want to read a novel," Susan said.

Use a period after the dialogue and before the quotation marks if the sentence is complete and followed by an action tag.

These are two complete sentences.
> "I want to read an exciting novel." Anne pulled a new book from the shelf.

Use a period after an action tag and before the dialogue.

These are two complete sentences.
> Anne pulled a new book from the shelf. "I want to read a novel."

Some writers feel that for dialect to sound authentic, they need to misspell words. This technique distracts the reader. Write in standard English so the reader understands perfectly what's being said.

- An occasional dropping of the letter "g" is permissible.
- An occasional "ya" instead of "you" is permissible.
- Avoid odd spellings.
- Fad or trendy speech patterns date your writing. Be sure this is the desired effect.
- Ethnic speech may insult your reader.

With foreign words or phrases, type it once in italics with the English meaning clearly identified. The second time, type it in regular font.

Use foreign words sparingly.

If in doubt, refer to *The Chicago Manual of Style*.

Vulgarity is a controversial topic in Christian publishing. It's a case of using realistic speech vs. potentially offending a reader. If you state a character swore, and the reader will understand the tension in the passage. This is an opportunity to incorporate figurative language without foul language.

> His outburst sounded like a sailor on steroids.

> I hadn't heard such language since my bar room days.

> "You worthless—" he cursed.

Read dialogue aloud. Text-to-voice software also allows you to hear how your prose sounds.

Eliminate extraneous words and write just what needs to be conveyed. Properly written dialogue moves the reader to laugh, cry, be angry, cheer — a whole gamut of emotions.

Pacing is key. If you need to speed up the scene, eliminate the gestures and action and let verbal communication carry the battle. If the pace needs to slow, add gestures, description, and action tags. A reader may skip the exposition, but she'll always focus on what's being said—the balance and rhythm of dialogue.

Ensure your dialogue is emotive, explosive, and ambiguous. You'll keep your reader turning pages.

Stretching

Compose a one-page passage of dialogue in each of these genres in which subtexting and body language play an integral role.

- Fantasy
- Romance
- Horror
- Suspense
- Historical
- Contemporary
- Contemporary Youth

Chapter 13 ~ Symbolism, Part I

*Chocolate symbolizes, as does no other food, luxury, comfort,
sensuality, gratification, and love.*
—Karl Petzke

The art of dance interprets life; it's a symbol of the highs and
lows of human emotion.

We can use symbolism to provide meaning to an object,
action, or thought with an abstract meaning beyond what we actually
describe. The action takes place on one level, while symbolism acts
on another to deepen the novel.

Writers often struggle with how to incorporate symbolism.
How does it fit into premise and theme? Does it heighten emotion?
Does it encourage the reader to see beyond the obvious? Is it part
of the story line? How does a writer choose a symbol? Is symbolism
critical for a successful novel?

In this chapter we'll discuss evocative language and why it's
an important tool in creating quality fiction—and how a writer can
incorporate this literary device.

Story is about a character with a goal to achieve or a problem
to solve. The character's journey is laden with difficulties, and while
attempting to put those problems behind her, she becomes attached
to "something"—a tangible item that takes on a psychological
meaning.

Symbolism touches the reader with subtle understanding of
theme and premise. Suddenly the weather, rushing water, a color, a
number, an item of jewelry, or the way the stars light up the night
mean something more—psychologically.

Since the beginning of time, storytellers have used symbolism to add depth to their tales. Consider the occurrence of a storm at a point in story where there are high emotions or conflict. Snoopy was right in borrowing from Edward Bulwer-Lytton: "It was a dark and stormy night." A transition from day to night, or spring to winter, could reflect a move from goodness to evil, from hope to despair. A river could represent the flow of life from birth to death. Flowers can project youth or beauty.

Eudora Welty said, "Symbols have to spring from the work direct, and stay alive. Symbols for the sake of symbols are counterfeit, and were they all stamped on the page in red they couldn't have any more quickly given themselves away."

Writers create their stories with character, plot, setting, dialogue, emotion, narrative, and so much more. Sometimes their own blood. Read back through that last phrase. What does "their own blood" mean to you? Hard work? Sweat that feels like blood?

The sentence came naturally, which is where all symbols are born. Every area of the writing process has the potential to add psychological meaning. By providing an evocative and emotional experience, we enable a reader to identify elements of story beyond the written word. She discovers a new level of appreciation because the symbol has attached itself to the characters—and the reader.

Not everything in a story is symbolic. A sunset can be merely a stunning display of color. A character enjoys Starbucks coffee. She fancies a particular model of car—and it means nothing else. The key is to incorporate symbolism without confusing the reader.

In *Word Painting,* Rebecca McClanahan says, "A symbol is a visible sign—an object or action—that points to a world of meaning beyond itself." That meaning is not directly stated, but through repetition the reader understands what it signifies to the character. In *Beginnings, Middles, and Ends,* Nancy Kress suggests a sensitive reader will conclude such a story with a sense of recognition.

A symbol can influence the overall dimension of story. In the premise, "Love conquers hate," the visual of a triumphant army overcoming incredible odds to claim victory can serve as motivation to create a powerful story line. The premise entices the writer to think outside her world, possibly opening her mind to develop the story in ways she has never considered.

In *Writing the Breakout Novel*, Donald Maass says, "The most effective pattern to follow is that of a single symbol." He points to the importance of the ring in Tolkien's *Lord of the Rings*, and how the story would not have had the impact if he had used several symbols.

Sometimes a writer, often a novice, becomes enamored with using symbols and peppers the manuscript with such elements instead of first creating a good story. Overuse dilutes what the writer wants to accomplish. The symbol becomes meaningless. For lasting impact, use the technique sparingly.

A symbol can underscore the spiritual realm of a story. That symbol doesn't have to be obvious. Perhaps a scarf a character's mother wore to church or a rocking chair her father used when reading the Bible. The key is to understand what the item represents psychologically. The reader may enjoy the story without recognizing your symbol. That's okay. But others will appreciate the added depth. Choose a character's name to signify who she is and her role in the story. The name must mean something, if only for you as writer. The stories rising from mythology, the Bible, and other cultures depict the importance of naming a child according to events, visions, culture, and family history.

A symbol of food can be used for a protagonist who sacrifices to feed the poor, or you can use food for an antagonist who gives for selfish reasons. In both instances, food represents the character's motivation. For one it is a vehicle to aid the hungry, for the other it is a vehicle of manipulation.

Characters may refrain from stating how they feel about a situation, but through our framing, the reader learns about their thoughts and emotions. A cleverly inserted symbol—a word or phrase that points to a deeper meaning—provides a subtle way for the reader to grasp the character's internal workings.

"A symbol means more than itself," Rebecca McClanahan says, "but first it means itself." She cites Crane's *The Red Badge of Courage*. The symbol is not courage (intangible) but the stain of blood (tangible). Although in this story the blood represents courage, it could mean something entirely different in another book.

James Scott Bell states, "From the start, we have a connection." The character(s) and the reader form an attachment to an object that no longer means only its original definition. Bell discusses Norman Maclean's *A River Runs Through It*, in which the setting is a river in Montana—and religion and trout fishing are considered one in the same. "The motif was literal at the beginning, symbolic at the end," Bell says. "It frames and defines the story."

A winding road may indicate a journey. A fork in the road may mean the need to make a choice. A straight road may represent determination or perseverance. Whether the choices are right or wrong depends on the character.

Symbolism in dialogue is another way to enhance the story's theme. Dialogue is birthed in character, which means that what she says, along with body language, demonstrates who she is. A character who stutters or uses flamboyant gestures or curses provides the reader with a glimpse into that character's life.

The things characters notice through their senses offer another source of symbols. What a character sees can mean so much, whether the object is physical or in the character's mind. In Charles Frazier's *Cold Mountain*, the mountain also represents the harshness of life as the characters struggle to survive.

In chapter six, we discussed creating an antagonistic setting. That also provides opportunities for strong symbolism. An encroaching forest fire can transform a fabulous vacation home into a death trap. Working for a prestigious company can become a source of evil, as in John Grisham's *The Firm*.

Then there's what a character hears. The call of a bird can be pleasant, unless the bird is a predator. A mother's voice normally signifies love and caring. But if a mother is abusive, the sound can represent impending danger.

As McClanahan says in *Word Painting*, what a character tastes can influence memory and perception. Any mother who's endured morning sickness will recall the foods that triggered an upset stomach.

Imagine a feast of pizza for a team of high school football players before the big game. What usually stands for enthusiasm and a commitment to win can change drastically if the players fall ill to food poisoning. Then the smell of pizza can provoke a lingering repulsive memory.

The sense of smell has incredible power. A writer introduces a woman with a distinct cologne. Whenever the male character notices that smell, he associates it with beauty, charm, and grace. But if the woman shuns him, he comes to despise that scent.

Touch can also infuse a story's with an array of emotions. As McClanahan says, "Touch, by definition, is an intimate sense…A well-written description that employs the sense of touch bridges physical and emotional distances." Consider the parent who disciplines a child with a time-out. When the parent retrieves the child to talk about the inappropriate behavior and to reinforce her love, she touches the child, both emotionally and physically. As McClanahan says, a person can be stimulated by what they see, hear, taste, or smell, but when a person is touched, the sensation invites intimacy.

In the next chapter, we'll continue our discussion. Until then, consider how you can add symbolism to your story.

Stretching

- If you have a symbol in your story, what is it? What does it mean to your character(s)?

- If you don't have a symbol, is there a possibility to include one? What might it be, and what could it represent?

- Your character has been given a medal for bravery for something she hasn't done. Write a short passage about how she views the medal.

Chapter 14 ~ Symbolism, Part II

Symbolism exists to adorn and enrich, not to
create an artificial sense of profundity.
—Stephen King

A dance not only provides entertainment, it also can usher in emotions that stem from experiencing the event—even if the emotions have nothing to do with the performance.

In the previous chapter, we discussed how symbolism adds richness to story. In this chapter, we'll explore some of the opportunities writers have to add that extra layer of meaning.

One way symbolism enhances fiction is through animals and nature. David Colbert writes, "Early Christianity reveals a Celtic pagan belief that a 'stag lost and regrew its horns, which was a symbol of resurrection and immorality.'" Roman historian Pliny wrote that a "stag was capable of destroying snakes." When the early monks sought to evangelize the Celts, they used the story of the stag to depict Christ's resurrection. This paved the way for C. S. Lewis to incorporate the white stag into *The Lion, the Witch, and the Wardrobe.*

Glimpses of nature are subtle means of leaving a message: a lone wolf, a struggling plant in a concrete city, mountains, a single tree in a field, a desert, and much more. The four seasons are often used to represent a person's life span. As a child is born and journeys through life, so do the seasons progress from spring to winter. A May-December wedding indicates the woman or man is much younger. A character experiencing the brink of adulthood may be symbolized by the summer of her life.

Colors and Numbers

As we discussed in chapter ten, we can use color to create mood and add meaning to a scene. The colors a character chooses for clothing, a vehicle, or those used in her home provide a subtle indication of her personality. In setting, the colors of a landscape or weather create a psychological effect that sets the temperature of the scene.

White signifies purity, peace, cleanliness, humility, light—all things right and good.

Red is the color of courage, love, seduction, pain, and agony.

Green is the color of life. It's vital to nature—a sanctuary or a symbol of growth. It can also signify money and wealth, envy, greed, and even corruption.

Blue is the color of the sea, sky, peace, harmony, calmness, coolness, and confidence.

Black can mean evil, death, power, and mystery. In Harper Lee's *To Kill a Mockingbird,* published in 1960 about the defense of a black man, black represents not only death, but also prejudice, hate, and evil.

Gray is strange psychologically. It stands between life and death, truth and falsehood, right and wrong.

Yellow represents joy, happiness, and hope—and cowardice. Dr. Dennis E. Hensley of Taylor University states, "Yellow is the only swing color. It can mean blindness, as in the biblical accounting of Paul's blindness on the way to Damascus, or it can mean enlightenment."

Purple can mean royalty, nobility, wisdom, or arrogance.

Brown stands for those things that are "of the earth." Numbers have always been viewed as symbolic.

Dr. Hensley states:

- One indicates wholeness.
- Three represents the Holy Trinity.
- Six means incompleteness, as 666 represents the Antichrist, the False Prophet, and Satan, who wants to be like God the Father, Jesus the Son, and the Holy Spirit.
- Seven indicates completeness, as in God finishing creation then resting on the seventh day.
- Twelve is the number of fulfilled judgment, as in twelve months in a year and twelve jurors deciding the fate of someone on trial.

By Genre

We can see the significance of symbolism through different genres. Horror, romance, suspense, western, historical, science-fiction, fantasy, and mystery novels use symbols to set the story's tone and voice. Just as symbolism in different genres requires tangible objects that take on abstract meaning, so does figurative language set the stage for story type.

Often using red and black, horror stories use symbolism to create an environment of death, evil, fear, savagery, and torture. Shadows and repugnant smells, along with rusty chains, knives, and ropes mark the horror sure to come. Horror stories draw their effect from words that evoke fear, dread, and pain. Alliteration, the hiss of "s," and soft and hard consonants all play a role.

Romance and many literary novels use flowers and the beauty of nature to represent how the characters feel about each other. All is filtered through the eyes of care and affection. These novels draw their symbolism from a poetic view of life and love. The phrasing is often lyrical, and the symbol resonates with intensity. The word choice feels graceful, sensitive, and contains a flowing rhythm. The metaphors and similes that evoke exquisite mental pictures often have a meaning of beauty.

Suspense novels can use a ticking clock, a dripping faucet, nature's fury, or other tangible items to create an edgy feeling. Such novels use specific words and phrases to keep the reader on edge, to keep the pages turning and the reader breathless. In his article, "Ten Rules for Suspense Fiction," Brian Garfield points out that the key in choosing symbols is to select the tangible item that represents a narrowing of space and time—then squeeze the time limit even more.[1]

Suspense authors may use objects such as an ambulance, a car that always refuses to start, or a watch that stops to intensify the suspense.

Westerns and historical fiction use objects familiar to the characters of the era to symbolize the story's essence. Barbed wire can indicate danger or an impending range war. A rusty star can mark a lawman who has sold out or a man too old for the job. Tumbleweed may indicate a restless character, and a curtain over a window may represent a woman's touch. These genres use language that combines culture and setting in creating passages that reveal the characters living in their time. How the characters earn their living, from the town sheriff to the local prostitute, influence the words they use—and thus the symbolism in their lives.

Science-fiction and fantasy often use terrain to establish not only symbolic meaning but also plot. Think of the role of water and its absence in the desert world of Frank Herbert's *Dune*. Bigger than life creatures can represent hurdles to be overcome. Daring attempts at heroics often indicate the insecurity in a character's life. Characters do not have to succeed to be a hero; they simply need to give their best. Science-fiction and fantasy also pull from a unique culture to establish figurative language. Often the writer is free to develop an environment and a vocabulary that reflects society. Creativity explodes in these genres and challenges the writer

---

1 Garfield, Brian. "Ten Rules for Suspense Fiction," *International Thriller Writers*. 1994. 23 Apr. 2008 < http://www.thrillerwriters.org/2007/01/ten-rules-for-suspense-fiction.html>

to develop symbols that fit the storyline, like a choreographer inventing new dance steps.

Mysteries invoke locked doors, bodies, missing weapons, and the traits of an unlikely sleuth to demonstrate the power of an unanswered question. This genre uses a crime, a sleuth, many clues, and red herrings. As Stephen D. Rogers states, "A red herring is something that appears to be a clue but in fact, it is not. Just as smoked herrings were used to lead fox hounds on a merry chase, red herrings give mystery readers false trails to follow." The figurative language generally involves clues to solve the mystery. These objects and the description can confuse the sleuth, but often not the reader. Word choice reflects the type of crime, the setting, and the clues.

Organic Symbolism

Symbols are everywhere. Perhaps you're reading this while sitting in a waiting room as the only passenger on a bus. Consider a dead-end street; a sign that states, "No shoes, no shirt, no entry;" or a teenager ignoring a parent.

Some writers carefully plan their symbolism, and cleverly place an object for its psychological meaning. But the best symbols arise from characters and their actions. The character views the symbol based on her experience and lures the reader also to look at it that way.

Once when I spoke to a book club about my novel *When the Nile Runs Red*, one of the members commended me on the use of symbolism. I had no idea what she was talking about, so—in hopes of putting together a literary response—I asked what was the clue. She pointed out my use of the Hummer. Then I knew what she was talking about. The setting was Southern Sudan before that war-torn country became independent. My hero had purchased his wife a Hummer to keep her safe, but I blew it up—signifying my hero's trust in the tangible instead of faith in God. I hadn't planned it as a symbol; it entered my story through the characters and plot.

For any writer, symbolism offers endless possibilities. You'll stretch yourself to create an artfully placed object that provides lasting meaning to the story. But its meaning and resonance for the reader is worth the challenge.

In the words of Stephen King, "Symbolism does serve a useful purpose, though—it's more than just chrome on the grille. It can serve as a focusing device for both you and your reader, helping to create a more unified and pleasing work."

Stretching

- What genre are you writing? How does the genre affect symbolism?

- In reading through the list of colors and referring to chapter ten on emotion, what color(s) will add psychological depth to your story?

- Write a short passage involving your antagonist's favorite color.

Chapter 15 ~ Exposition, Narrative Summary, and Internal Dialogue

Narrative is linear, but action has breadth and
depth as well as height and is solid.
—Thomas Carlyle

Novel writing is like a dance team who, with their individual personalities, work together to entertain us. We don't see the many layers of perfected steps and creativity that go into a choreographed number, but those items must be added for the dance to succeed. Understanding where each dancer fits into the routine takes effort and hours of sweat. So while they're drenched, let's establish the difference between exposition, narrative summary, and internal dialogue so we can understand how these literary techniques may fit into your story.

Writers often question the use of exposition, narrative summary, and internal dialogue. They understand these devices can make a story drag, yet they have value. Because one of the first lessons a writer learns is that "telling" brings rejection from agents, editors, and readers, she may assume she should delete anything that isn't dialogue. This chapter will explain these techniques and how to use them.

Readers want to see action unfold as it is happening. They are disappointed when a writer fails to allow them to be part of the story, as though someone threw a lavish party and the reader wasn't invited. But is there a place for exposition, narrative summary, and internal dialogue?

The Trouble with Exposition

A common misuse of exposition is the information dump. In effect the writer hits the story's pause button and unloads what she feels is vital information. So she tells the reader all she knows about a subject from her research. This authorial intrusion not only annoys the reader, but it also demonstrates a writer's me-first attitude. Masses of exposition do not serve your story as an engine additive. Take your dump truck filled with exposition and park it where your reader will never find it.

Identifying Exposition

Can you pick out the exposition below?

Susan eased into the chair facing Karen's desk. "You wanted to see me?"

"You're fired." Karen lifted her chin. "I told you when I took over as supervisor that I'd look for a way to get rid of you."

, Susan coaxed her lunch back into her stomach, a Swiss cheese and ham on rye from the new deli across the street. The establishment had given all the employees a free sandwich, but the bread was hard and the cheese was old. "I just landed a two million dollar account."

Karen sneered. "I'll take the credit." She nodded at the door where the security guard stood. "Please escort Susan to her desk. Make sure she retrieves only her purse before removing her from the building. Walk her down the unpainted hallway, where the painters are using a semi-gloss paint from Sherwin-Williams."

"I want to talk to the CEO."

"Send him an email."

The CEO didn't provide his email address. Life's unfairness had gone on for years. Susan's past demonstrated one failure after another. The first one was in kindergarten when her mother held her back because she couldn't read.

The next door neighbor told her she was stupid, and her dad said they'd have to move. Two weeks later, she spilled milk at the table when her parents had guests for dinner. Three days later, she tripped over the dog, and the animal howled and bit her. Her grandmother accused her of stealing money from her purse. Susan had a temper tantrum.

And the exposition in the scene below:

"Hey Mom, I really appreciate your helping me bake cupcakes for Tommy's kindergarten class for his sixth birthday." Susan handed her mother a freshly brewed cup of coffee that she'd prepared with Starbucks' new blend just before her arrival.

Mom took a sip of the black coffee, and Susan waited for her response. "Perfect. Thanks for inviting me to your new house on Elm Street where you've lived for only three months,"

"Oh, we love the four thousand square feet and new furniture that we bought when we moved in. Would you mind pulling out the cupcake tins, you know the ones that hold the cupcake papers that are in the pantry?"

Mom set her coffee cup on the counter and pulled out the cupcake tin. "These are dirty. Mind if I wash them?"

Susan gasped. The horror of her mother finding a soiled cupcake tin was more than she could bear. What if Mom told her friends? What if the school found out and wouldn't let Tommy serve the cupcakes to his friends? "I'm so sorry. I'll scour them with Comet and rinse them in bleach so they will be clean and disinfected for Tommy's birthday cupcakes that he wants to take to school tomorrow for his kindergarten class in honor of his sixth birthday."

Mom picked up her coffee cup. "Susan, get a life." (And so should we if we write like this.)

I'm sure those scenes gave you a laugh, but hyperbole can be a good teacher.

Backstory can cause the same problems as exposition if not used properly. The events that happen before chapter one drive the character's motivation. But release that information in bits and pieces, when required by the plot. Blended in properly, backstory helps readers understand the motivation behind your story.

Sidestepping Summary

The purpose of narrative summary, also known as summary or narration, is to summarize events that aren't vitally interesting but still need to be included. Although "show, don't tell" is a writer's motto, minor happenings should be revealed in the most effective way: clearly and succinctly.

Before including it, make certain a section of narrative summary is needed. Keep your reader engaged by showing your character struggling to achieve a goal and changing in the process. Long passages of summary cause a reader to skim and move on to action—or possibly even stop reading. So be clear and brief.

Still, short passages of narrative summary can play an important role:

- To cover time
- To clarify how one point affects another
- To state minor happenings needed for the storyline
- To provide a change of pace when action has been high and suspenseful for several scenes

Write narrative summary in the POV character's voice, weaving it into story, then move quickly into action. Summary tends to be non-emotional, and emotion keeps a reader turning pages. Used sparingly, the device can provide information that advances the story without disturbing the reader.

The paragraph below uses narrative summary:

> Three years passed before Susan saw Karen again. Her ex-boss scooted into a church pew in front of her.
>
> "How are you?" Susan hoped her smile looked more sincere than what she truly felt.
>
> Karen's lips trembled. "My mother had a heart attack. She didn't make it."

Effective Internal Dialogue

Internal dialogue—also called introspection or interior monologue—refers to the conversation inside your character's head while she reacts externally. Using it allows you to place a full spectrum of character emotion onto the page, ensuring the passage is rich and credible. Written in the character's POV, it's intimate, often pondering matters the character would never say.

This technique does not lie, unless the character is mentally unstable. Because the internal conversation is gut-wrenchingly honest, it hooks the reader into the privacy of the character's soul. It's easier to write in first-person, because you're conveying the story through a single point of view.

During high-stress scenes, a character can be on an emotional high and think irrationally—or she can remain calm and focused. Through internal dialogue a reader learns much about the character's goals, problems, emotions, scars, and spiritual dilemmas.

Writers once used italics to set apart internal dialogue, but publishers are moving away from this. Italics force a reader to make a mental adjustment, running the risk of tossing the reader out of the experience. I prefer keeping the reader in the story, vicariously living every moment through a character.

This example weaves dialogue with the character's thoughts. Note how the first-person narrative reveals the subtexting.

> "Karen, why not relax and have a drink?" Dad lifted a glass filled with amber-colored liquid. "Lighten up. So your mom's dead. Good riddance."

I needed to get away, some place where I could breathe. The stench of tobacco laced with alcohol brought back painful memories. I swore when I was seventeen that I'd never step inside this house again. Never be subjected to his foul mouth or his beatings. Yet, here I—

"Cat got your tongue?"

I forced a smile. "I'm fine. Just a glass of water will do."

"Still too good to drink with your dear old Dad?" His slurred words were only part of the poison. How had Mom put up with him all these years? I used to despise her for not taking me and running, but her faith kept her a prisoner. Made me wonder if her heart attack was a blessing. I had no idea where her afterlife had taken her, but it had to be better than living with Dad.

Do you know more about Karen now? From this short passage we understand her ruthlessness when she fired Susan. Her backstory doesn't justify her actions, but it provides a reason for her actions—and builds reader sympathy.

Stretching

- Look at a scene in your story. Are there blocks of exposition longer than just one sentence? Rewrite that scene.
- Choose another scene. Do you see ways you could use narrative summary to move past less important events?
- Choose a scene with action and dialogue. Can you find a way to use internal dialogue to show the real character?

Chapter 16 ~ The Rhythm of Pacing

—Stephen King

Pacing reminds me of a dancer who builds momentum before leaping into the air with beauty, grace, and purpose. Her rhythm is flawless. Her delivery exquisite. She tells a story that one cannot resist because she varies each movement. The dancer understands that repetition lulls the audience to sleep.

In the well-crafted novel, rhythmic pacing keeps the story alive and moving through scenes and sequels that leave the reader eagerly turning pages.

Scene (action) and sequel (narrative) have distinct purposes. Action is faster, heart-throbbing, and heart-wrenching. The writer uses tension and conflict—with the element of surprise—to engage character emotion. Narrative is a deliberate literary technique to slow the story so the reader can identify with what's happening to the viewpoint character. Continuous action doesn't allow a reader to get inside the POV character's head. Overload can quickly set in. But too much narrative causes the reader to skim so she can get back to the action.

Sounds simple, right? Then in the middle of our novel, a critique partner points out that our story has screeched to a halt.

How can writers pace their story to keep it appealing? Readers will forgive a lagging story for only so long before they close the book. In chapter eight we discussed ways to speed up dragging portions. Look at those suggestions again, along with the four suggested plot questions. Rate your scenes from one to ten for importance. If a scene dips below eight, you have work to do. Tighten. Tighten. Tighten. Look for the element of predictability, and make necessary edits.

Genre and Pacing

Genre is an area where pacing affects the characters, story line, setting, dialogue, and theme.

Romance novels are built on the premise of two unlikely people finding a lasting love that nudges them to make a lifelong commitment. The romance portion plays on the wants, needs, and fears of a possible relationship. Each offers what the other has, but the idea of making a commitment is frightening. Is each character willing to fight for love? Are they willing to sacrifice for the other? What threatens to keep them apart? Strong emotions are present, along with conflict and tension. The success or failure of the novel depends on how well a writer paces this growing relationship.

Historical fiction is often set in a time when life was slower. Pacing must be realistic, but don't let the story creep across the page. Readers of this genre want to know about the culture—dress, home life, social graces, and language. Weave these tidbits expertly

Two Simple Rules

✔ Scenes, also called action or cause, speed up pacing. Readers love this. They eagerly read to see what predicament the character will get into next.

✔ Sequels, also called reaction or effect, slow down pacing. Use sparingly.

throughout the story without reverting to exposition or lengthy narrative.

Suspense novels use the ticking clock technique to keep the pace moving with intense action that builds on each scene—until the climax bursts onto the page, claiming heroes and exposing villains. Get a metronome, a device used by musicians that clicks a steady tempo. As you type, increase the beats per minute. This works—if it doesn't drive you crazy.

Science fiction and fantasy novels, as well as other forms of speculative fiction, are often quests that prove the hero or heroine's mettle. While you want the reader to understand the setting, culture, language, and character motivation, slower segments must still move the story to an action-filled scene.

Conflict and tension are allies of good pacing. Add emotive conflict, and the character is motivated for future scenes.

A few tips to keep the pace flowing

Action scenes use short sentences or phrases. Narrative takes the time to complete a thought, explore emotions, weigh options, plan actions, or manipulate others in the increasing need to reach a goal.

Action	"Hurry. They're gaining on us."
Narrative	The memory of the kidnapping still keeps me awake nights. Just when I think the nightmares are over, it happens. The countless hours in the psychologist's chair meant nothing when I saw the knife…heard his voice.

Write action scenes that keep the reader holding her breath and still begging for more. We want our stories to be addictive.

Pacing is not about extending action scenes but accomplishing a purpose.

Write short narrative scenes. I heard an editor say she wished all books could be scene and no narrative. What she meant was lots of action with a sprinkling of narrative—for pacing.

Sometimes you need to hit delete on a sequel portion and send the character into another scene—or even change to a different POV character.

Word choice is important to genre, character, increasing pace, and slowing it down. Short words, sentences, and paragraphs peak action while longer passages slide into narrative.

> She slapped me.

Or

> My face stung from her open palm. The remainder of the evening was spent in a blur, my heart ablaze with what how she'd betrayed me—again.

You can slow down pacing by using a different viewpoint. This pushes the reader to make an adjustment and form a bond with a new character or return to an already established relationship.

Write only what the viewpoint character experiences. No time to smell the flowers unless your character's picking them and is stung by a bee.

Is a scene stagnant, devoid of conflict and tension? Consider having it take place off stage, then have the POV character consider the outcome in narrative.

> She'd stood me up for the third time. Made me feel like a fool, especially when I saw her snuggle up to her ex. I'm finished.

Don't cheat the reader by failing to use every ounce of emotion and action to build higher stakes.

Give the character a time limit to accomplish a goal, then slice it in half.

Build pacing with the what-if principle. What is the worst possible thing that could happen to the viewpoint character? Make a list and brainstorm a scenario crammed with surprises.

- What if Susan forgot to turn on the light in her aunt's backyard?

- What if Susan fell into the pool?

- What if Susan didn't know a water moccasin was in the pool?

- What if Susan didn't know the snake had killed a man that night?

- What if Susan touched the man's body?

- What if Susan tried to climb out, but someone pushed her back?

You control the dance of character and plot. Speed up the pacing and fill the reader with excitement, then slow it just long enough for your reader to grab her blood pressure medication before another dynamic scene. Take charge of the dance, and keep your readers coming back for more.

Stretching

- Find a middle scene in your novel or write a scene you know will be in the middle. Cut it in half. Are the character's actions predictable? If so, kill your darlings.

- Examine the scene again. Convert it to one-paragraph of narrative summary. Which format—action or summary—best propels your story?

Chapter 17 ~ The Writer's Voice

All stories have a curious and even dangerous power. They are manifestations of truth—yours and mine. And truth is all at once the most wonderful yet terrifying thing in the world, which makes it nearly impossible to handle. It is such a great responsibility that it's best not to tell a story at all unless you know you can do it right. You must be very careful, or without knowing it you can change the world.
—Vera Nazarian

When I was four, my mother took me to my first dancing class. I wanted to watch before I joined in. I didn't understand that I had to participate to be a part of the class, even if I made a mistake. A writer who wants to develop a unique voice can't simply read novels, she must write.

Does the subject of voice make you want to run? You're not alone. Explanations run the gamut from the way a writer pens her prose to bigger-than-life characters who attract us with their view on life. Voice is everything the characters experience and express according to their traits and the writer's individual style. A writer chooses unpredictable characters, both in actions and in dialogue, and establishes a voice that draws us into the story.

A writer's voice is her fingerprint, a way for a reader to identify style. It can't be developed by studying a textbook or taking a writing course. Each writer has a unique way of stringing together words and sentences, a subconscious activity stamped with personal style, word choice, originality, and passion for the project.

We develop our voice over time—by writing, polishing our craft, and knowing our characters. It's much like our unique conversational style, but with a strong additive: the character's voice. That means no two characters ever quite sound alike. A strong writer's voice doesn't overpower the character, but hooks the reader's attention and refuses to let go.

I like how Donald Maass describes voice: "not only a unique way of putting words together, but a unique sensibility, a distinctive way of looking at the world, an outlook that enriches an author's oeuvre…An original. A standout. A voice."

Your ability to dive into character and create an adventure strengthens your voice. In establishing that voice, weigh each word choice. Is it succinct and descriptive? Use strong verbs and vivid nouns, the ones your character would use. Have you chosen the best word in the character's voice, one you're comfortable with? A writer's genre also influences word choice. A lot to think about, but when you tune out the critics and write the story of your heart with a character you love (or love to hate), voice will be in your fingertips.

**Ask About Your Voice
Have a Reader Describe your Voice**

Ask these tough questions:

- ☞ **Is there a rhythm?**
- ☞ **Is it distinct?**
- ☞ **Do all the sentences sound the same?**
- ☞ **Are the characters exceptional?**
- ☞ **Do you hear the character's voice or just the writer's?**

I went through several stages of forming my voice while following rules, not following rules, then allowing my writing to morph into my voice. When I concentrated on good writing and put the guidelines into perspective, aside, my voice came. Note that what is appropriate for style, format, genre, and publisher guidelines is not the same as exploring and finding your unique writer's voice.

As Thomas Merton said, "Not all men are called to be hermits, but all men need enough silence and solitude in their lives to enable the deep inner voice of their own true self to be heard at least occasionally."

The following areas are important to me. While they may not become part of your writer's voice, they'll give you an example of the subconscious development that is necessary to establishing your voice.

- I'm a bare bones writer. I don't like to read paragraphs of description, so I don't write them. I use humor sparingly and always in character. I can be dark—or I can be flirty. Sometimes a character requires a little more of what I avoid, so I have to weigh my preferences with what the character's telling me—then mix the two. Sometimes all it takes is a single word or phrase to accomplish voice.

- I detest exclamation marks. I will stay up all night rewording scene and dialogue to eliminate that little bat and ball from the end of sentences. I prefer using word choice, characterization, and the scene's mood to convey emotion. But if an editor believes it's the best choice, I will present my case…and together we'll make a decision for the sake of the story.

- I use only said as a dialogue tag. It's an invisible word. The only other tag I might consider is whisper.

- I don't use asked as a dialogue tag. The punctuation mark and the syntax show the sentence is a question. Why insult the reader by telling them twice it's a question.

- I want my writing to be understood immediately. That means not sending readers to the dictionary. Clarity with distinctive nouns and verbs is more important than a word's number of syllables.

- I don't use semicolons or colons in fiction.

- I believe the use of italics for internal dialogue tosses the reader out of the adventure.

- I emphasize style, word choice, originality, and passion for the project to establish individuality.

Don't be afraid to be you. A distinct voice means having the confidence to allow your personality to shine through your story. Outstanding writing comes from composing one sentence after another. When a reader can say that only you could have written that story, then you have established your voice.

Stretching

To help you develop your voice, work through each question and exercise.

- What do you respect about your favorite writer's work?

- What makes her work distinctive?

- What writing rules and guidelines are important to you?

- What writing rules and guidelines do you consistently break?

- What genre do you write? If you write historical romance and your voice is dark, you need to alter your voice.

- List ten items you are passionate about. For the next ten days, spend fifteen minutes a day writing about each item. Close your eyes and simply create, whether a story, an essay, a poem, a screenplay, a blog, or a song.

- Use text-to-voice software to hear your work read aloud. Listen to the rhythm. As a listener, are you engaged?

Chapter 18 ~ Building Your Editing Muscles

You write to communicate to the hearts and minds of others what's burning inside you. And we edit to let the fire show through the smoke.
—Arthur Polotnik

A dancer advances her career by practicing. Hours of it. She knows her performance will not improve unless she's committed to her art. A novelist improves her craft the same way: the art of writing one word after another until the story has been told in the best possible way.

Have you ever read something you wrote one year ago, six months ago, or yesterday and cringed? Word choice, descriptions, characters, plotting, or setting screamed back at you. We are always learning the craft. Our calling is not limited to merely creating a draft manuscript; we must perform edits and revisions. Our readers deserve our best, which means we cut the flab and build muscle into our writing.

Consider revision an exciting challenge—an adventure to make your writing more powerful. Look forward to it, because revision and editing provide an opportunity to make your creation better—and eventually the best.

Edits and revisions mean hours of laboring until we have a sculptured piece we are proud to submit. "Unwillingness to revise," Sol Stein says, "usually signals an amateur."

I've met novice writers who said not one word of their work could be changed because God had given them the manuscript.

Obviously they didn't need an editor. Don't be unteachable or you'll never succeed in this business.

Penelope Stokes calls revision a humbling experience. But how much better for the writer to catch any poor grammar, plot failures, and inconsistencies than an editor who tosses our work back at us.

I highly recommend *Self-Editing for Fiction Writers* by Browne and King. You can conquer bad habits and strengthen weak areas by following their guidelines. We all have areas in which we can improve.

Approaches to Revision

Don't try to revise while you write. Finish a scene, a chapter, or even the entire story before switching to editor mode. Creating a story uses the left side of your brain. Revision uses the right. While writing the first draft, you're learning about the story and its characters.

Only you can determine how many drafts your story needs. A critique group or partner can help you see blind spots.

My routine is simple. Perhaps it will help you.

- I try to write strong copy.

- Each morning I reread what I wrote the previous day and make edits. I make notes after each scene indicating what clues or threads I need to address before I complete the book. Some novelists use a project journal.

- After the first doorway or at about 20,000 words, I read the story to ensure I'm being true to my premise and characters. I edit and make notes.

- Midway, after I've written a critical turning point, I repeat the process.

- When I've completed the first draft, I read the story for flow, often doing intense editing. This is when I begin sending chapters to my critique partners.

- I let the story sit as long as possible, ideally two months. There is a measure of perspective that comes only from allowing our manuscripts to rest.

- I use text-to-voice software for each chapter. This allows me to hear the story, the flow of the plot, characterization, and sentence rhythm. Sometimes I catch grammar and punctuation inconsistencies.

- I read the story one more time on screen—and then in hard copy. Maybe more if I'm not satisfied.

- A writer knows when she has achieved her best work.

Some writers prefer editing from hard copy, using various highlighters to point out problems. I simply scribble notes on my printouts with a pen. You may prefer a systematic approach, even doing separate reads for character, plot, dialogue, and narration. No matter your approach, apply it thoroughly.

Editing Goals—Items I search for during self-editing

Active Voice

Activate your sentences. Often "to be" verbs indicate a passive sentence. Exemplary writing uses vivid nouns and strong verbs. "As" and "-ing" words can also mark a passive sentence.

Avoid Clichés

Create your own metaphors and similes—or give old ones a twist—using your character's traits and voice.

Beginnings

Be sure your story begins with the lead character's name and her current situation?

Chapter Hooks

Develop the best sentence to hook your reader into your story.

Characterization

Ask these questions about your hero, heroine, or protagonist.

- What about them do you like or dislike?
- Is there a positive and a negative trait that doesn't belong?
- If you were to spend a vacation with the hero or heroine, what about the character would appeal to you?

Ask these questions about your villain or antagonist

- Is the character truly evil or badly behaved?
- What is the one trait that gives the character redeeming quality? As Sol Stein says, no villain can attract victims unless he has charm, charisma, or wealth.

Chronology

Use a calendar to keep track of your chapters.

Try http://calendarhome.com/tyc/#calendars

If your book is a period piece, make sure the historical aspects are factual.

Conflict and Tension

Reread every page, paragraph, and line to be sure conflict and tension are present.

Consistency

Check spelling, especially names to be sure all are the same. Determine if numbers will be written in numeric form or spelled out and check for uniformity.

Cut Extra Words

Be clear. Be willing to condense. Never use two or more words if one word works.

Dialogue

- All dialogue should be clear and tight.
- Verify that all dialogue punctuation is correct.
- Determine which dialogue lines need a tag and or a beat.
- Find and eliminate adverbs
- Review each dialogue to be sure the words are in character.

Emotional Conflict

Evaluate every paragraph and every line to see if you have included emotional conflict.

Examine Plot

Ask the four crucial questions regarding each scene (see chapter seven).

Genre

Decide if your genre is clear. Consider how the story will feel to the reader (creepy, brooding, inspirational)?

Grammar

Ascertain if you need a grammar guide; if so, invest in one. Look for dangling participles and misplaced modifiers. Verify all punctuation.

Plot

Ask if you have kept your plot tight. Find any holes in the plot and tie up all the threads.

Pronoun Preference

Check all pronouns to determine if the reader will immediately know what noun the pronoun stands for?

Redundancy

Avoid repeated phrases. Don't insult the reader by telling something more than once.

Scenes

Rate every scene from one to ten. Delete or rewrite any below eight. Each scene should propel the story, building conflict and tension. Make sure the first and last lines are strong. Are the transitions smooth?

Sensory Perception

Check each scene for the presence of the five senses.

Series Order

Place one-syllable words first: beans, cabbage, and tomatoes instead of huckleberries, pear, and a banana.

Count the number of words. List the shorter items first: He enjoyed green beans, deep fried onion rings, and buttered corn-on-the cob.

If all the items have the same number of syllables, consider their place in the alphabet.

Or consider chronological order, obvious sequence, familiar sequence, and unintended modifiers.

Sometimes the way we're used to hearing items contradicts these guidelines. If the list doesn't sound right, change the order.

—Lunch, dinner, and breakfast should be breakfast, lunch, and dinner.

—Cream and peaches should be peaches and cream.

—The bees and the birds (alphabetical sequence) should be the birds and the bees.

—Gold, myrrh, and frankincense should be gold, frankincense, and myrrh.

Setting

Research more than you think you will ever use. Fictitious towns are best. Map out your town ahead of time, filling in street names, residential, business, etc. How can the setting be antagonistic?

Vary Sentence Length

Read sentences aloud to hear the rhythm.

Word Choice

Confirm you've chosen the best words. William Shakespeare said, "Suit the action to the word, the word to the action."

Unintended Modifiers

Make sure your modifiers modify what you intend.

The bank of the long and winding river made a great site for a picnic. (Correct)

Long and winding, we shared a picnic on the river bank. (Misplaced modifier)

Look for Writer Termites

That	If the sentence makes sense without "that," it can be deleted.
Which vs. that	Use "which" for a nonrestrictive clause. (The clause is not needed; it's additional information.) Use "that" for a restrictive clause. (The clause is needed for the sentence's meaning.)
"There" or "It"	Rewrite any sentences beginning with "There" or "It"
Adverbs and Adjectives	Find each adverb and adjective to determine if it is necessary.
"However" or "Suddenly"	Delete all uses of "however" and "suddenly."
Do a global search for —ly with a space after it —ly with a period after it	Eliminate these words ending in -ly if possible.

Is your story filled with muscle? If not, head to the weight room. Your readers will thank you, and your story will dance.

Stretching

- What's your personal method of editing? What suggestions from this chapter might help you?

- Print your story's first chapter. Using the guidelines in this chapter, edit your manuscript.

Chapter 19 ~ The Tango of the Writing Life

The writing life offers exciting challenges. But it's also a lonely calling: the writer, the computer, and God. We have goals and deadlines, and we're constantly working to improve our craft. Professionals instruct us to join writing groups, find critique partners, attend conferences, and stay involved with social media—all while we labor over our writing. So how do you juggle the demands of writing with your life beyond the keyboard?

Boo Birds

Boo birds sit on the power lines of our lives and drop their stuff. Critique partners, readers, editors, family members, friends, and professional critics all have an opinion of what we do. And they are free with their questions and advice.

- How much money have you invested in your hobby?
- Why aren't you published?
- I read your story. Good thing you have a job to pay the bills.
- You're out of control. We all agree you're eccentric, bizarre, and need meds.
- You're spending way too much time on something that won't happen.
- Give it up. This is bad.

132

In weak moments, we ask ourselves if the goal of publication is worth the sacrifice. Maybe we need to go back to a normal life, whatever that is.

How do you continue when encouragement is scarce? Reach back to why you started writing. Do you view your passion for communicating the written word as a calling? Is your desire to share your story with readers more powerful than the opposition from critics? If you cannot not write, you need to ignore those boo birds and keep working toward your goals.

Conferences, Writing Groups, and Critique Partners

Writing conferences help you learn new skills from professionals who know the craft, the publishing business, and marketing and promotion. In a few days, you can arm yourself with new techniques—and find motivation to continue. Some conferences provide face-to-face meetings with mentors, agents, and editors. Meeting other writers who share the same joys and trials helps you feel you're not alone. Many of those new friendships continue long after the conference.

Writing groups require a commitment from each member to give back. For those writing for the Christian market, the Christian Writers Guild, www.christianwritersguild.com, specializes in training writers on all levels. The American Christian Fiction Writers, www.acfw.com, offers an online community, a national conference, and local groups that meet monthly.

A critique partner can help us refine our manuscripts. But finding the right partner is like searching for a new doctor. Not everyone is a good fit. Look for someone with the same or higher skills who writes in your genre. Critique partners who meet in person develop mutual trust and often become good friends. Online critiquing helps battle the time crunch. I've done both. If a situation stops working, for whatever reason, graciously resign. A sense of responsibility is not a reason to continue in a critique relationship that no longer has value.

Establish ground rules with a potential critique partner.

- ✔ Will you meet online or in a scheduled place? Is Skype an option?
- ✔ How many pages will you exchange?
- ✔ How many writers will be in the group?
- ✔ Will the critiques be a line edit or a content edit?
- ✔ What will be the turnaround time?
- ✔ How will you handle a critique partner who consistently fails to submit her work?

Industry

The publishing world is not for the fainthearted. To survive, writers must keep adding to their skills. We take a deep breath and open our minds to the changes in the publishing world so we can adapt with optimism.

- ✔ Publishers add new genres and eliminate others.
- ✔ Publishers merge and change ownership.
- ✔ Methods of publication change.
- ✔ Payment formulas become more complex.
- ✔ Self-publishing becomes more tempting.
- ✔ Writers must take a greater role in marketing and promotion, especially with social media.

The one thing that never changes is the value of quality writing. That's our number one job. We must write a novel that's not just good, but outstanding. Nothing else matters. If we are to stay in the game, our personal goal of writing better every day becomes a necessity.

We'll never fully understand how some writers are blessed with publication while others—equally committed to quality writing, professionalism, marketability, platform, and meeting a publisher's needs—struggle to have their work read by agents and editors. But a writer in tune with the publishing industry understands persistence is her best partner.

We write—and we continue to submit—because we are writers.

Pay it Forward

Is there something more a writer can take from this book? Could there be a surprise additive to the list of how to succeed in the world of publishing?

I believe so. In fact, I know so.

To be blessed, one must be a blessing to others. It's simple. Biblical too. Has a more successful writer taken you under her wing? Did that writer teach you technique and recommend how-to books, workshops, and conferences? Was she your nightmare editor and your best cheerleader? Did she:

- Take a personal interest in you?
- Brainstorm ideas and various ways to present your story?
- Challenge you to write stronger?
- Push you into social media?
- Make you cry and then encourage you to keep writing?

If you had a mentor who loved you enough to not let you write garbage, you are fortunate. I had a mentor, and now I am one.

Some veterans are willing to help a new writer who is committed to developing the craft. Those people make time to ensure another rises to her full potential. Both the mentor and the writer make sacrifices: time and effort. Rewrites. Trudging through line edits.

If I ever think I'm too big to help a new writer, God may think I'm too small for publication.

The Greeks understood the dynamics of mentoring. Nestled deep in their mythology is the story of aging Mentor who imparted wisdom to Telemachus, the son of Odysseus. The name came to mean someone who shared wisdom and knowledge with someone less experienced—a faithful and wise adviser.

Think about your part in helping new writers. Do you want to teach others? Such a commitment partners with one to educate ourselves in the craft. Time restraints and family and job responsibilities may prevent you from participating. That's okay. Your current role may be simply to learn more about the craft. There are other ways to give back, such as a critique group, a monthly writers group, or a commitment to pray for new writers.

Kay Arthur said, "You have been created by God and for God, and someday you will stand amazed at the simple yet profound ways He has used you even when you weren't aware of it."

If supporting and encouraging writers is in your future, prepare for the rewards of blessing others.

In the resource section, you'll find guidelines for face-to-face and online critique groups.

Priorities

Many times our other priorities stop us from writing. Writers who find themselves juggling life and achieving little success with their commitments and goals will abandon their calling. The answer lies in understanding principles for organizing our lives.

Take inventory of what is important to you. Christians seek to place God on the top rung. Our relationship with the Author of creation must come first, or we'll never experience peace of mind.

Second should be our family. These are the people entrusted to our love and care. Life is about relationships, not how many books we've written or how many times we've hit the bestseller list. What counts is leaving a living legacy by showing our loved ones how much they mean to us.

Third is our day job. Writers often look forward to when they can write full-time. Before you make that leap, ask yourself these questions:

- Can I write outstanding manuscripts with the pressure of knowing that if the story doesn't sell, my family doesn't eat?

- Can I afford to buy medical insurance for my family without the benefits of a full-time position?

- Will I earn as much or more through writing than what my day job provides?

The fourth priority is your friends and your commitment to them. Ignoring friendships for the sake of reaching any goal is selfish. Balance is the key.

Fifth comes your writing. In chapter one, we discussed finding time to write. This includes every aspect of working as a writer. Consider your schedule and commitments, then insert a time. My pastor says, "Obey immediately." That doesn't mean we shake off our responsibilities until after we finish our blog.

Professionalism

Because writers are in the limelight, we have to look and act professional at all times. Whenever I walk to the mailbox, I look my best. Laugh if you must, but think about your neighbors or those driving by your house or the UPS driver who all know you're a writer. Begin to develop good habits that ensure you present yourself appropriately. Your dress, makeup (if you're a woman), and up-to-date hairstyle mean you've left an excellent impression.

Business cards are your introduction. Just as you greet others with a smile, so should your business card. Keep the card simple with your name and contact information. A photo provides an added touch, if it's been taken by a professional photographer.

Platforms are an important marketing tool. If yours is weak, choose speaking topics that reflect your uniqueness. Have a website designed that expresses your genre and themes. Develop your speaking abilities through Toastmasters, CLASSeminars, or a college class. At first, you may be speaking for coffee and cookies, but you're building a resumè. Create a blog in which you offer something to readers—and collect email addresses.

Social media offer excellent ways to reach out to others. Choose what works best for you. But realize social media is about them, not you. And remember, everything you post remains in cyberspace forever. So think before you type.

You represent the next generation of writers. You are the one who will answer the challenge of reaching others through the power of story. Readers are waiting for you to pen the next word … and the next. *The Dance of Character and Plot*—where will it take you?

Resources

On the following pages are some templates to help you with writing and critiquing. Use them freely to advance your skills.

Character Sketch

Moral premise of story _______________________________
____
____

Story title _______________________________

Genre _______________________________

Character name _______________________________
Meaning of Name _______________________________
Temperament Type _______________________________

Temperament type explanation _______________________________
____
____
____
____

Character's physical story problem _______________________________
____

Character's psychological problem(s) _______________________________
____

Character's Outer Landscape
____
____

Birth date _________________Nickname _________________________

Height ___________________________Weight___________________

Complexion____
Race____

Nose ____
Ears____
Eye color and shape ____

Body type ____

Positive distinguishing features ________________________________
____

Imperfections____

Physical illnesses or afflictions ________________________________

Characteristic gestures/mannerisms ____________________________
____
____
____

Home—Where and describe ___________________________________
____
____

Education and where received _________________________________
____
____

Occupation ____
Salary ____

Vocabulary ____

____

Skills, abilities, and talents ___________________________

____

____

Interests/hobbies ____________________________________

____

Social status ____

____

Sense of humor _______________________________________

____

Joys ____

____

Pets ____

____

Favorite meal ____

____

Establishing Character Motivation

Family background/birth order/lineage including ethnicity________

____

____

____

Political views _______________________________________

____

____

Religious affiliation ______________________________
____
____

How much does faith play in the character's life? ____________
____
____
____

What is your character's spiritual turmoil? ______________
____
____

Type and number of close friends _________________________
____
____
____
____

Bestfriend____
____
____

How do your character's family and friends view him or her?
____
____
____

What about life does your character appreciate? ____________
____
____
____
____

If your character could be or do anything in life, what would it be?

____

____

____

What person or persons does your character admire? ____________________

____

____

____

Why? ____

____

____

____

Things that make your character uncomfortable or embarrassed

____

____

____

____

Traumas or scars from the past _____________________________________

____

____

____

What makes your character angry? ___________________________________

____

____

____

How does your character handle anger? ______________________________

____

____

____

What are your character's fears? ___________________________________
____
____
____

What is your character's most painful experience? _________________
____
____

What is your character's biggest triumph? _________________________
____
____

What are your character's weaknesses? _____________________________
____
____

What are your character's strengths? ______________________________
____
____

Twelve Tips for Writing Strong Character-Driven Dialogue

Characterization

Who is your character? What makes him tick? What has been her life journey? Your role as a writer is to take the time to write the back story so you will know what influences the way the character speaks.

Be a Good Wordsmith

This means showing and not telling. Avoid -ly words that reveal you haven't mastered powerful and vivid nouns and verbs.

Genre

Romance, sci-fi, suspense, western, fantasy, mystery, historical, and contemporary use dialogue to reflect the story's genre and theme.

Conflict and Tension

Conflict and tension pace your dialogue through believable conversations that show different personalities responding to what is going on.

Dialogue Tags and Beats

Stick to the tag "said" when writing dialogue. Use it sparingly, only to denote who is speaking. Beats are actions that surround dialogue. A tag is not necessary when a beat shows the reader who is speaking. The goal of dialogue is for the reader to know who is speaking by the character's choice of words, emotions, and body language—without the use of a tag or a beat.

Clear, Concise, and Credible

These three Cs of writing tight dialogue also apply for any type of writing.

Body Language

Up to 90 percent of our communication comes through body language. Use this valuable tool to show character emotion.

Emotive Conflict

The reader expects the protagonist and antagonist to have heated conversations, but also use this tool to show that friends can have conflicting emotions.

Picky Punctuation and Gritty Grammar

How you punctuate dialogue may make the difference between a sale and a rejection. No editor wants to be buried by errors. Get a grammar and punctuation guide, and use it.

Silence

Silence is an effective technique in dialogue. Use gestures and body language to relate what the silent character is feeling. What counts isn't what's said, but the effect of what's meant.

Subtext

What does the character really mean? Dialogue that means only what is said fails to mirror character emotions.

Panning for Gold

In writing witty dialogue you must sift through the words, actions, and body language to find the rich nuggets that keep the reader turning pages—and the sales up.

Four Essential Plot Questions

1. What is the POV character's goal or problem?

2. What does the POV character learn that he/she didn't know before?

3. What backstory is revealed? (Avoid backstory, flashbacks, or protagonist's flaws for the first approximately 50 pages)

4. How are the stakes raised?

Backstory

Inspired by
Writing the Breakout Novel Workbook
by Donald Maass

- What happened in your character's life up to age twelve that affected who she is today?

- What happened in your character's life from ages thirteen to twenty that affected who she is today?

- What happened in your character's life from ages twenty-one to thirty that affected who she is today?

- What happened in your character's life one year before the story opens?

- Six months?

- Six weeks?

- Twenty-four hours?

- One hour?

- Ten minutes?

Knowing Your Story

- What is the premise of your book?

- What is the hook sentence of your book?

- What is the takeaway for the reader?

- Who is your target audience?

- What are three unique features of your book?

- How is your book different from anything else out there?

- Did you write the back cover copy of your book?

- Why would you buy your book?

Guidelines for Face-to-Face Critique Groups

- Determine how many writers in the group.
- Establish a meeting place.
- Establish manuscript format.
    - 1 inch margins
    - Double spacing
    - 12 point Times New Roman or Courier New font
    - Header with automatic page numbering
- Establish length of submitted manuscript.
- Number the lines of the submitted manuscript.
- Understand each member's genre.
- Submit polished writing as though each member is an editor.
- Writer brings copies of manuscript for each participant.
- Someone other than the writer reads the work aloud.
- Writer is permitted a two minute lead-in before work is read.
- Writer does not speak during the reading.
- Each writer is given 15 minutes of critique time.
- Participants will not interrupt the speaker.
- Always thank the person who has given the critique.
- Don't take suggestions personally.
- In making constructive criticism, use the Oreo method. Begin with a compliment, make appropriate suggestions, then close with encouragement. Honesty is critical, but unkind remarks are forbidden. Harshness does not make a better writer.
- Make specific suggestions. General comments do not help the writer.
- Address punctuation, flow, content, and credibility.
- Critique according to writer's ability/level of expertise.
- Each member of the group is responsible for adhering to guidelines.
- If a writer doesn't submit her own writing, she shouldn't critique another's work.
- Enjoy the experience! This is a time to admire and respect your peers.

Guidelines for Online Critique Groups

- Determine how many writers in the group.
- Establish manuscript format.
  - 1 inch margins
  - Double spacing
  - 12 point Times New Roman or Courier New font
  - Header with automatic page numbering
- Establish length of submitted manuscript to be critiqued.
- Establish a time when manuscript is submitted.
- Establish deadline when critiques need to be returned to all participants.
- Understand each member's genre.
- Submit polished writing, as though each member is an editor.
- Always thank the person who has given the critique.
- Don't take suggestions personally.
- In making constructive criticism, use the Oreo method. Begin with a compliment, add suggestions to make the manuscript better, then end with encouragement. Honesty is critical, but unkind remarks are forbidden.
- Make specific suggestions. General edits or comments do not help the writer.
- Address punctuation, flow, content, credibility.
- Critique according to writer's ability/level of expertise.
- Each member of the group is responsible for adhering to guidelines.
- If a writer doesn't submit her own writing, she shouldn't critique another's work.
- Enjoy the experience! This is a time to admire and respect your peers.

Suggested Readings

Character, Emotion, and Viewpoint by Nancy Kress
Conflict and Suspense by James Scott Bell
Dialogue by Gloria Kempton
Dynamic Characters by Nancy Kress
Elements of Fiction Writing: Conflict and Suspense by James Scott Bell
Fiction Attack! by James Scott Bell
Fiction Writing Demystified by Thomas Sawyer
Goal, Motivation, and Conflict by Debra Dixon
How Fiction Works by Oakley Hall
How to Grow a Novel by Sol Stein
I Know What You Are Thinking by Dr. Lillian Glass, Ph.D.
Mastering Point of View by Sherri Szeman
On Writing by Stephen King
Plot and Structure by James Scott Bell
Revision and Self-Editing by James Scott Bell
Self-Editing for Fiction Writers by Renni Browne and Dave King
Story by Robert McKee
Techniques of a Selling Writer by Dwight Swain
The Art of Character by David Corbett
The Art of War for Writers by James Scott Bell
The Chicago Manual of Style by The University of Chicago Press
The Elements of Style by William Strunk Jr. and E .B. White
The Fire in Fiction by Donald Maass
The First 50 Pages by Jeff Gerke
The Moral Premise by Stanley D. Williams
The Power of Body Language by Tonya Reiman
The Writer's Little Helper by Jim Smith
Word Painting by Rebecca McClanahan
Writing Dialogue by Tom Chiarella
Writing for the Soul by Jerry B. Jenkins
Writing the Breakout Novel by Donald Maass
Writing the Breakout Novel Workbook by Donald Maass

Suggested Websites

Meyers-Briggs Personality Testing

http://www.humanmetrics.com/cgi-win/JTypes2.asp

OneLook Reverse Dictionary

http://www.onelook.com/reverse-dictionary.shtml

The Bookshelf Muse: The Emotion Thesaurus

http://thebookshelfmuse.blogspot.ca/p/ emotion-thesaurus.html

10,000-Year Calendar

http://calendarhome.com/tyc/

About the Author

Award-winning author DiAnn Mills is a fiction writer who combines an adventuresome spirit with unforgettable characters to create action-packed, suspense-filled novels. DiAnn's first book was published in 1998. She currently has more than fifty books published.

Her titles have appeared on the CBA and ECPA bestseller lists and have won placements through the American Christian Fiction Writer's Carol Awards and Inspirational Reader's Choice awards. DiAnn won the Christy Award in 2010 and 2011.

DiAnn is a founding board member for American Christian Fiction Writers and a member of Inspirational Writers Alive, Romance Writers of America, and Advanced Writers and Speakers Association. She speaks to various groups and teaches writing workshops around the country. DiAnn is also a Craftsman Mentor for the Jerry B. Jenkins Christian Writers Guild.

She and her husband live in sunny Houston, Texas.

Visit DiAnn's website: www.diannmills.com

Follow DiAnn on

www.facebook.com/diannmills

twitter.com/diannmills

23992490R00085

Made in the USA
Lexington, KY
01 July 2013